GOOD ★ SPORTS

GLENN STOUT

FROM HARDSHIPS TO CHAMPIONSHIPS

sandpiper

HOUGHTON MIFFLIN HARCOURT
BOSTON NEW YORK 2013

Library of Congress Cataloging-in-Publication Data
Stout, Glenn, 1958–.
From hardships to championships/ by Glenn Stout.
p. cm.
ISBN 978-0-547-88735-7
1. Baseball players—United States—Biography—Juvenile literature.
2. Baseball players—United States—Conduct of life—Juvenile literature.
I. Title.
GV865.A1S819 2013
796.3570922—dc23
[B]
2012023943

Manufactured in the USA
DOC 10 9 8 7 6 5 4 3 2 1
4500395929

For everyone who has ever lost—
and then learned to win.

CONTENTS

INTRODUCTION

THERE ARE SOME THINGS ABOUT our lives that we can't control. While growing up, none of us is in control of where we live or under what conditions, or who our parents are or what our family is like. In fact, the differences between us are what make each of us distinct individuals.

Some people grow up in nice neighborhoods but feel neglected and ignored. Others might grow up in poverty and be surrounded by love and support. Some children might be raised by wonderful parents who work too hard to pay attention to their children, or by single parents who do a terrific job. And some might be raised by people who have trouble with drugs or alcohol or who are ill and cannot care for them. Everyone's circumstances are different.

Those circumstances can sometimes make life hard for a young person, but it doesn't need to be that way forever. The best part about growing up is that as we do, each of us can take control of his or her own life. No matter how difficult a person's upbringing might be, it is still possible to live a productive life. By finding something you love to do and working hard at it, it is possible to overcome all sorts of difficulties.

The players profiled in this book were able to use baseball to help them overcome neglect, poverty, drug and alcohol abuse, and even mental illness. Babe Ruth was neglected by his parents, refused to go to school, and was sent away. Jimmy Piersall suffered from mental illness. Ron LeFlore grew up using drugs and stealing, and he spent time in prison. Joe Torre was terrorized by his father. Torii Hunter grew up poor, surrounded by gangs, with a father who was addicted to drugs.

Yet these men all managed to find a way out of their circumstances, to get help, and, through baseball, a game they loved, to turn their lives around. Despite the difficulty of their childhoods, each still managed to have a wonderful career and a productive, positive life.

Each of us who finds something we love to do and works hard at it can do the same. You might not make it to the major leagues, but you can still be happy and successful.

That's part of being a Good Sport.

BABE RUTH: FROM ST. MARY'S TO THE HALL OF FAME

NEARLY ONE HUNDRED YEARS AFTER Babe Ruth first played in the major leagues, he is still considered one of the best players in the history of baseball. After starring as a pitcher for the Boston Red Sox, and as a slugging outfielder for the New York Yankees, Ruth changed the game forever. He became baseball's first great home run hitter, thrilling fans with his long, dramatic home runs and leading the Yankees to four World Series titles. At one time he held the record not only for the most home runs in one season, sixty, but for the most home runs in his career, 714.

But Babe Ruth was more than just a great player. He also became one of the most beloved athletes of all time. He played the game with the joy and exuberance of a child and sometimes acted like an overgrown boy. Kids loved his big laugh, his big smile, and his big stomach. He never seemed happier than when he was surrounded by a bunch of children clamoring for his autograph.

Yet when Babe Ruth was growing up in Baltimore, Maryland, no one would ever have imagined that he would be great at anything or beloved by anyone other than a member of his own family. Ruth himself once wrote, "I was a bad kid." Yet despite growing up in circumstances that would have crushed the spirit of most children, he discovered that the game he loved could help turn his life around. Baseball helped save him.

Babe Ruth was born George Herman Ruth Jr. on February 6, 1895, the first child of George and Kate Ruth. His friends and family called him Little George to distinguish him from his father, who was called Big George. The Ruths had seven more children, but only one, Babe's sister Mary, survived infancy. For most of Babe's childhood his mother was ill and confined to bed.

Big George worked hard, but he rarely had much money. As a young man, he tried his hand at a number of different professions, but when Little George was six years old, Big George opened a restaurant and bar in Baltimore. The family lived above the saloon in a small apartment.

It was hardly the way for a young boy to grow up. His father worked at the saloon from early in the morning until late at night, when barroom brawls sometimes spilled into the street. After his sister Mary was born, George's mother had her hands full taking care of an infant, and she had little time for George, who grew up with very little supervision. He was often left to roam the neighborhood in the company of other boys.

Although George and his young friends spent some of their time playing games such as baseball and football, the neighborhood around the waterfront offered plenty of opportunities for adventure and mischief. The wharves were always an attraction for the boys. There were boats loading and unloading supplies, and there were sailors from all over the world.

It didn't take long for George and the other boys to get into trouble. They banded together for protection from older kids. They were all poor, and they stole from food stands and grocery stores and committed small acts of vandalism. Neighborhood shopkeepers kept an eye out for George and his friends and chased them through the streets when they believed they had stolen something.

When George stayed home, he usually spent his time hanging around at his father's saloon. While still a very young boy he picked up some bad habits, such as chewing tobacco, smoking, using bad language, and drinking. Neighbors complained to the police about the amount of time Little George was spending in the saloon. They told the police, "It's no place for him."

One time when George was in the saloon, he saw his father leave the cash drawer unattended. He waited until no one was looking, then reached in and stole a dollar — a great deal of money at a time when most people were lucky to earn fifteen dollars a week. Then he dashed out of the saloon and met up with his friends. He shared his wealth by buying ice cream for everybody.

Unfortunately for George, his father soon discovered that the cash drawer was a dollar short, and he heard that George had been seen eating ice cream. When George came back to the saloon, his father confronted him. The boy confessed, and his father grabbed him by the collar and marched him down to the cellar beneath the saloon, where he beat him with a horse whip.

The punishment didn't change George's behavior. He was angry with his father over the whipping and became even more defiant, stealing from the drawer whenever he had the chance.

George should have been in school every day, and each morning after he woke up and got dressed, that's where he was supposed to go. But his parents couldn't walk him to school, so as soon as he was out of sight, he headed in the opposite direction. Instead of learning to read and write, he was learning how to become a criminal.

George's parents cared about him, but they just didn't know how to care *for* him. Yet they knew that if he remained on the street all day, he would never learn, and without an education he would never amount to anything. They had both seen young boys turn to a life of crime and end up in jail or killed. Neither wanted that life for their son.

The Ruths knew they had to do something before it was too late for George to turn his life around. They went to a local justice of the peace and had their son judged "incorrigible" and "out of control of his parents." Then they managed to get George committed to the St. Mary's Industrial School for Boys.

St. Mary's was operated by the Catholic Church for orphans, juvenile delinquents, and boys who were simply poor and neglected. The school was staffed by priests, known as Xavierian Brothers, who wore long, flowing robes. The goal of the school was to provide an education for young boys, give them religious instruction, and offer job training so that when they became young men, they would become productive members of society. More than eight hundred students between the ages of six and twenty-one stayed at the school.

On the morning of June 13, 1902, George and his father boarded a trolley car together. George had no idea where he was going, but when they got off the trolley, he looked in wonder at the massive granite building. St. Mary's main building was nearly five hundred feet long and several stories tall, and it had an enormous tower in the center. When George stepped through the front door for the first time, he was terrified. His father explained to him that he would be leaving him behind. George thought he was a tough kid, but when his father left, he began to cry. He was seven years old.

Although he did not know it then, that was the most important day of his life. Had he not attended St. Mary's, George Ruth never would have become Babe Ruth. Although he occasionally tried to see if he could make it back home with his parents, he never left St. Mary's for long. He would spend the next twelve years there, the most important years of his life.

The Xavierian Brothers viewed teaching and taking care of the boys as part of their commitment to serve God, and they took their duties seriously, even living at the school with the boys. They tried to treat the students as if they were all members of the same big family, and they cared about the boys and were able to give them the kind of time and attention few of them had ever received before coming to St. Mary's. If anyone needed this, it was George Ruth.

It was difficult at first. As he later recalled in his autobiography, "I honestly don't remember knowing the difference between right and wrong." He had done whatever he wanted, whenever he wanted, without a thought about how his acts might affect other people. Because he had skipped so much school, George couldn't read or write or do basic arithmetic. The brothers had a big job ahead of them.

Every boy at St. Mary's was woken up at six o'clock each morning when the bell in the bell tower rang; they had to wash, dress, and attend church before breakfast. Next came five hours of school, a two-hour break for lunch and recess, and another two hours of school or work training. In the late afternoon and on the weekends there was time to play sports and compete on various school teams, that is if the boys completed their schoolwork and stayed out of trouble. After dinner they had some time to read and do schoolwork before turning in at 8:15 p.m. There was hardly any time to get into trouble.

George hated it. He couldn't stand being told what to do all the time. He returned home several times, but inevitably he started skipping school again and soon had to be sent back to St. Mary's. Each time he returned, instead of being angry with him, the brothers welcomed him back. Soon St. Mary's became his home.

Each brother at the school was assigned a group of about a dozen boys to supervise. George was placed in a group under the direction of Brother Mathias, who was in charge of discipline at the school.

Brother Mathias stood over six feet six inches tall and weighed nearly three hundred pounds. He was so big he rarely needed to raise his voice. One look from Brother Mathias was often enough to tell a student he had done wrong. Yet despite his size, Mathias was gentle. He treated all the boys fairly and was well liked. Many of the boys stayed in line not because they feared him, but because they didn't want to disappoint him.

Mathias had seen many troubled boys come through St. Mary's. He realized that the biggest reason George was in trouble all the time was because neither of his parents had the time or energy to pay much attention to him. George wasn't bad. No one had ever taught him how to behave. Mathias was determined give the boy a chance.

He spent time with George, getting to know him and earning his trust. After all, in some ways George had never had an adult care for him before. At first he was shy and afraid, but Mathias started pulling him out of his shell. He discovered that although George was undisciplined, he was also bright, engaging, and full of energy. George soon realized that he needed Brother Mathias and that the priest was his friend. "He taught me to read and write, and he taught me the difference between right and wrong," Ruth later said of Mathias. "He was the father I needed and the greatest man I've ever known."

Mathias took George under his wing. He gave him special help with his schoolwork so he could catch up with the other boys. He also got him started in trade school. George went to work in the school's tailor shop, learning to make shirts, cutting the cloth from a pattern and then sewing it together on a sewing machine. Mathias taught George that he had to live by the rules and work for everything he received.

//

George wanted to please Mathias and the other brothers, and he worked hard. He quickly became a fine tailor and later bragged that he could sew a shirt in fifteen minutes.

He also worked hard because he knew that if he got his work done early, he would be allowed extra time to play sports, which he liked more than anything else at St. Mary's.

The school had two large yards, one for younger boys and one for older boys. The school's athletic director, Brother Herman, supervised the school's athletic programs. Nearly every boy at school played sports, and the school offered programs in football, soccer, handball, boxing, wrestling, and other activities.

But no sport at St. Mary's was more popular than baseball. Many of the brothers were big baseball fans, and the school supported more than forty teams of players organized by age. The best players made the school team that played other schools.

George soon discovered that he loved baseball. Every afternoon Brother Mathias played with the boys, hitting them fly balls. George watched in wonder as Mathias tossed a ball into the air and then, swinging a bat with only one arm, hit long, soaring fly balls from one end of the yard to the other. He loved watching Mathias hit, and he dreamed that one day he would be able to hit the ball just as far.

Baseball changed George's life. When he discovered the game and learned to trust Brother Mathias, he suddenly had reasons to go to school and stay out of trouble. From that moment forward, his behavior began to improve.

Mathias worked with him on his baseball skills just as much as he did on his studies, using baseball to motivate him in the classroom. George improved rapidly in both areas and tried to imitate Mathias in everything he did, even teaching himself to copy Mathias's stylish handwriting. On the ball field George was a left-handed thrower and batter. He earned a reputation as one of the best hitters his age at the school, and he also had one of the best arms. Soon he was playing on half a dozen teams, spending several hours each weekday and most of every Saturday and Sunday playing baseball. Big and strong for his age, he usually played catcher, using his powerful arm to keep base runners from stealing.

However, there were still times when George would act up, like most boys. In one game, the pitcher for George's team started to struggle, giving up hit after hit. Instead of supporting his teammate, George began to heckle him and laugh.

Brother Mathias watched silently for a few moments, then stopped the game. He approached George and asked, "What are you laughing at?" George didn't know what to say. Mathias handed him the baseball and said, "All right. You pitch."

"I don't know how to pitch," said George.

Brother Mathias acted as if he were surprised. "You must know a lot," he said, "to know your friend isn't any good." Then his voice turned serious. "Go out there and show us how it's done." Mathias believed that George would struggle, and he hoped to teach him a lesson.

George was embarrassed. He knew he had done wrong, and even worse, he had disappointed Brother Mathias. The only thing he could do now was to try his best.

He stood on the mound awkwardly as the other boys giggled with anticipation, expecting him to fail. But when he wound up and threw the ball, it streaked right over the plate. With each pitch he got a little more comfortable, and soon he was buzzing fastballs past hitters and even trying out a few curve balls. George learned his lesson, but at the same time, he and everyone else at St. Mary's learned that he was a pretty good pitcher. From that moment on, George was both a pitcher and a catcher. And he stopped making fun of other players.

By the time George was sixteen years old, he was nearly full grown and the best ballplayer at St. Mary's. He had little competition at the school, and the Brothers trusted him enough to allow him to play for local amateur and semipro teams. George was soon as successful outside the walls of St. Mary's as he was within, and over the next few years he earned a reputation as one of the best amateur ballplayers in Baltimore, with a sweeping curve ball, a potent fastball, and a powerful bat. His name began appearing regularly in Baltimore newspapers.

But George wasn't quite done pitching for St. Mary's. The Xavierian Brothers also ran a nearby college, Mount Saint Joseph. When George was nineteen, the brothers from both schools got together and, of course, started talking baseball. Brother Gilbert, the baseball coach of Mount Saint Joseph, began bragging about their team, particularly pitcher Bill Morrisette. In response, Brother Mathias and Brother Herman started bragging about George Ruth. Soon the brothers were arguing about who was better. To settle the argument, they decided to schedule a game between the two schools.

The game was played at Saint Mary's, and the whole school turned out to watch. A big crowd from Mount Saint Joseph also accompanied their team to the game. The college boys thought the teenagers from St. Mary's didn't have a chance.

But there was a special guest in attendance. Although accounts differ, either Jack Dunn, the owner and manager of the Baltimore Orioles, or one of his scouts was in the crowd.

Dunn's Orioles were one of the best minor-league teams in the country, and he was always on the lookout for new ballplayers, particularly pitchers. In fact, he had already seen Bill Morrisette pitch, was impressed, and hoped to sign him to a contract at the end of his college season. But several people had also told Dunn to take a look at the St. Mary's pitcher named Ruth, so Dunn either decided to attend the game and watch both young men or he sent one of his scouts. Either way, it was hard to believe that a schoolboy and his team could outplay a college team with an experienced pitcher like Morrisette.

But George Ruth was no ordinary schoolboy. He was already taller and stronger than most men, and during his years at St. Mary's he had played thousands of innings of baseball. Brother Mathias had seen to that.

George made the college players look foolish. Against his sidearm curves and fastballs, they were almost powerless. Batter after batter walked back to the bench, head down and dragging his bat, another strikeout victim.

The game wasn't even close. George and his teammates shut out Mount Saint Joseph, winning 6–0. Out of twenty-seven possible outs, George struck out an amazing twenty-two men.

Jack Dunn didn't wait long. He soon went to see Brother Paul, the school superintendent, and asked to meet George. The two men and the schoolboy spent several hours talking. Dunn wanted to sign George to a contract to play for the Orioles, but Brother Paul explained that George wasn't yet free to leave St. Mary's. George's mother had died several years earlier, and afterward George's father had agreed to allow the school to become George's legal guardian. He was supposed to stay in their custody until he was twenty-one years old.

At the same time, Brother Paul didn't want to hold George back from doing something he clearly loved to do, which could earn him a good living. And he knew that George had come a long way since he first arrived at St. Mary's as a young, foulmouthed delinquent. There had been bumps along the road, but George had made tremendous progress as a student and as a person.

Dunn visited St. Mary's several more times, getting to know George and watching him play before he and Brother Paul reached an agreement. When George turned nineteen, Brother Paul would arrange for Dunn to become his legal guardian, allowing him to sign a contract to play baseball.

In February 1914, just a few days after George's nineteenth birthday, Dunn returned to the school and was made George's legal guardian. He then signed him to a contract for the 1914 baseball season worth $600—$100 a month. George would stay at the school until the end of the month and then join the Orioles for spring training.

On his final day at St. Mary's, George packed his few belongings in a battered suitcase and reported to the school's office to be released. He shook hands and said goodbye to the brothers who had taken such good care of him. He was excited but also a little afraid. But he knew that he was a far different person from the "bad kid" who had first entered St. Mary's twelve years earlier.

Before he left, Brother Mathias spoke. "You'll make it, George," he said.

Then George Ruth walked out of St. Mary's toward the rest of his life.

It didn't take George Ruth long to succeed. At spring training with the Orioles, the veteran players started to call the rookie "Babe," and the name stuck. Babe Ruth became one of the Orioles' best pitchers, and before the end of the season he had made an appearance with the major-league Boston Red Sox and finished the season with a minor-league team in Providence, Rhode Island. He made the major leagues for good in 1915, winning eighteen games and helping the Red Sox win the World Series that year. Over the next few seasons he was one of baseball's best pitchers, and he helped the Red Sox to world championships in 1916 and 1918 as well. In 1918 he began playing outfield and was sold to the New York Yankees after the 1919 season. In New York he became one of the greatest hitters in baseball history and helped make the Yankees a championship team.

By the time he retired, after the 1934 season, he held the major-league record for most home runs in a season, with sixty in 1927, and most home runs for his career, with 714. He was also the most popular and beloved figure in the game. In 1936 he was one of the first five players elected to the National Baseball Hall of Fame.

JIMMY PIERSALL'S BATTLE AGAINST MENTAL ILLNESS

ON JANUARY 15, 1952, JIMMY PIERSALL appeared to be living out his boyhood dream.

Movie-star handsome, he was twenty-two when he became a top prospect for the Boston Red Sox. He was already considered one of the best outfielders in professional baseball when the Red Sox noticed his quick reflexes and strong arm and in the off-season decided that he had the skills to play shortstop. They asked Piersall to come to their spring training facility in Sarasota, Florida, more than a month before the start of regular spring training for some special instruction to learn the new position. The Red Sox player-manager, Lou Boudreau, and general manager Joe Cronin had both been star major-league shortstops. Cronin was already in the Hall of Fame, and in 1970 he would be joined there by Boudreau. Each man thought that Jimmy could be a big star, and both planned on working with him personally. Jimmy's future looked bright, and many observers thought he might one day become a Hall of Fame ballplayer himself.

Piersall and his wife, Mary, were already parents of a young daughter, and Mary was expecting another child in a few months. Jimmy's life seemed just about perfect.

When Piersall arrived by plane in Sarasota, he took a cab from the airport to his hotel. Then he got out of the cab and walked toward the front door.

Eight months later, he woke up in a mental hospital in Westborough, Massachusetts, strapped to a bed. He didn't know where he was or how he had gotten there. Moreover, he remembered almost nothing that had happened since the day he arrived in Sarasota.

Yet as Jimmy would soon learn, he was in the process of turning his life around. Even though he was still hospitalized, the young man who was now trying to piece together the previous eight months of his life was far more fortunate than the young man who seemed to have it all just a few months earlier. As Jimmy later said bluntly, "Probably the best thing that ever happened to me was going nuts."

That's because it was not until he was diagnosed with mental illness that a lifetime of pain and agony began to be replaced with one of peace and understanding.

Jimmy grew up in Waterbury, Connecticut. His father was a housepainter and his mother a housewife. Times were often tough, and his father was often out of work, but the Piersalls took good care of their son.

He was a bundle of energy, and there was nothing he liked better than playing catch with his dad in the small backyard behind their apartment. In particular, Jimmy enjoyed making catches that made him jump into the air or leap over something. In his mind the wood fence that surrounded the yard was like the fence in a ballpark. During each game of catch, Jimmy robbed imaginary hitters of dozens of base hits.

He loved baseball and shared his father's dream that he would one day become a major-league ballplayer. Although his father was strict and could be impatient, there was always time for the game. They would play catch together for hours or listen to radio broadcasts of his dad's favorite team, the Boston Red Sox. Sometimes they went together to a hill overlooking a nearby park and watched games. Jimmy's father took baseball very seriously and was always telling his son to pay attention, saying, "You must learn the game backwards and forwards." For Jimmy, baseball became very serious. He wasn't allowed to goof off or fool around, or his father would become very angry. As Jimmy admitted later, "I would do anything to avoid his anger. He set his own rules, and I tried hard not to disobey them, for I lived in fear of his wrath."

To Jimmy, sometimes it seemed that nothing he did on the field was quite good enough for his dad. If he got two hits, his father wanted to know why he hadn't gotten three, and when he got three, his father wanted him to get four. When Jimmy's friends were celebrating after a game, Jimmy worried that he hadn't played well enough.

When he was in second grade, he came home one day to find his father sitting alone. Jimmy called for his mother, but no one answered. His father told him that she had simply "gone away." He promised that she would be back, but didn't offer any other explanation.

Jimmy was confused. Eventually he learned that his mother was having mental and emotional troubles — what people sometimes refer to as a "nervous breakdown" — and had to be hospitalized. For the rest of Jimmy's childhood his mother was in and out of the hospital. When she was at home, there were times when she behaved normally, but at other times she seemed to do everything at full speed. Then she would sob and cry for no apparent reason. Sometimes she behaved erratically. Once, she walked into the street without paying attention to the traffic rushing by. Jimmy had to run into the street and get her safely to the other side.

His mother's condition and his fear of his father made Jimmy afraid and anxious. He began to worry about his mother constantly and about other things, too, such as whether his friends really liked him and if his homework was good enough or what would happen if he dropped a ball while playing catch with his father, and a thousand other things. He felt as if he could never relax and he always had to stay busy. Even as a young boy he had a variety of jobs: helping the milkman every morning, delivering newspapers and groceries, and pumping gas at a service station. The money he made helped his family pay the bills, but staying busy kept Jimmy from worrying too much.

In his spare time he played baseball and basketball as much as possible on youth leagues and school teams. He was quick and wiry and played with a focus and intensity unusual for a boy his age. In fact, he sometimes drove his teammates to distraction. He worried about *everything* that happened in the game. When Jimmy was playing, he was constantly yelling at his teammates, telling them where to throw the ball, arguing with the referees and coaches, and racing all over the court or the field, giving orders to everyone.

For Jimmy, the games never ended. Every night he replayed each game over and over in his head, berating himself for small mistakes, staying awake for hours until he finally fell asleep. Although his friends would tell him he was usually the best player on the field, he never felt good enough. Later he described the way he felt at the time — as if he were on a merry-go-round that kept spinning faster and faster, as if there was no way he could get off or slow it down.

As Jimmy reached high school, his worries increased. His parents were older, and he realized that they would soon depend on him to help take care of them. He worried about making enough money to do so and what he would do if they became ill.

One day when Jimmy was fifteen years old, he got a headache. He thought at first that his sinuses were bothering him, but the headache never went away. Despite being in terrific pain every day, he rarely complained and soon learned to live with it.

He didn't realize it at the time, but his headaches, hyperactivity, and inability to sleep were warning signs of possible mental illness. Today a teacher or a counselor would probably notice and try to get him some help, but when Jimmy was a boy, there was little understanding of mental illness. Everyone thought he was just different, or eccentric. As long as he did well in school and succeeded at sports, no one thought there was anything seriously wrong with him. When Jimmy's behavior was discussed, people simply considered him "high-strung" or "tightly wound." No one thought he was sick.

When he was at Waterbury's Leavenworth High School, Jimmy turned out to be one of the best athletes in the state. He played baseball not only on the school team but on amateur teams against adult players twice his age. He even led the Leavenworth basketball team to the Connecticut state basketball championship and then to the New England championships at the Boston Garden.

The team met Durfee High School of Fall River, Massachusetts, in the finals. Thousands of fans were screaming as the game was tied 44–44, with only three minutes left to play. During a time-out, Jimmy's team huddled by the side of the court.

The coach started to speak, but it was the kind of situation in which Jimmy found it impossible to keep quiet. He seized command from his coach in the Leavenworth huddle, barking out orders to his teammates like a general. "Jimmy was very determined and very focused," said one of his teammates later, "saying 'Give me the ball and I'll get you a score.'"

Then, as one newspaper put it, Jimmy began to play "like a savage animal." Over the final three minutes he was all over the court, grabbing rebounds, chasing after every pass and stealing the ball, then streaking toward the basket. He scored the final seven points of the game to lead his team to a 51–44 victory and finishing with twenty-nine points of his own. The *Boston Globe* described him on the front page as "one of the best all-around players seen here in many years." And basketball wasn't even his best sport!

What made his performance even more remarkable was that his father had recently suffered a heart attack and was in the hospital. As Jimmy later recounted, winning the game didn't even make him happy. He was worried sick about his father's heart condition and his mother's emotional health.

Jimmy had been offered a scholarship to play baseball in college, but after his father's heart attack he decided that his family needed him to work. There was no baseball draft at the time, so as soon as he graduated from high school, he was eligible to be signed by a professional team.

A number of different teams were interested, among them the Boston Braves, the Detroit Tigers, the New York Yankees, and the Brooklyn Dodgers. The Braves, in fact, offered Jimmy a $20,000 bonus to sign. He was thrilled. He thought that would solve all his family's problems. He would be able to take care of them financially and could finally stop worrying about everything.

But Jimmy's father pointed out that according to the rules then in place, if Jimmy accepted a large bonus, he would have to join the Braves in his second year whether he was ready for the big leagues or not. As his father put it, he might "rot on the bench" and never reach his potential. Besides, Jimmy's father wanted his son to play for the Red Sox. A week later the Red Sox offered Jimmy a three-year contract for $4,000 a year, including a $2,000 bonus. When Jimmy asked if they would pay for his father to get a health checkup and they agreed, he decided to sign with the Red Sox.

He should have been happy. After all, he was going to

become a professional baseball player. Instead, he found more things to be concerned about. Now he worried about what would happen if he got hurt or wasn't good enough to make the major leagues.

Jimmy played semipro baseball and worked in a factory for the rest of the summer, then refereed basketball games until it was time to travel to Florida for spring training. But on the long train ride from Connecticut, he was obsessed with thoughts of failure. Not until he actually took the field was he able to relax a bit. When he was playing, he usually focused so much on the game that he rarely thought about much else.

Even Jimmy didn't expect to make the Red Sox in his first year of pro baseball, and after spring training he was sent to play on the Red Sox Single-A farm team in Scranton, Pennsylvania. He played well, met his wife, Mary, and the following year moved up to Triple-A Louisville, Boston's best minor-league team, one step from the big leagues. Although Jimmy still had headaches every day and was still distracted by constant worrying, at the end of the 1950 season he was called up to the Red Sox and made a great impression. The next spring, he made the team in spring training as a backup outfielder.

Manager Steve O'Neill told Jimmy that he might not

play very much, which didn't make him feel any better about sitting on the bench every day. After only a few days in the majors he went to his manager and asked, "When am I going to get into a ball game?"

O'Neill told Jimmy he would eventually get a chance, but for now he just wanted him to watch. But Jimmy couldn't stand not playing. It simply made him too anxious. He told his manager he'd rather play in the minor leagues than sit in the majors.

O'Neill was puzzled—no one ever *asks* to go to the minor leagues—but a few days later the Red Sox sent Jimmy down to Louisville. Despite doing well there, he occasionally had to sit out so the team could play someone else at his position. Jimmy began to worry that the Red Sox wanted to get rid of him, and he begged them to send him to another minor-league team where he could play every day. This time he was sent to Birmingham, Alabama, Boston's Double-A team.

Finally allowed to play every day, Jimmy had a fabulous year, hitting .346 and catching nearly every fly ball in sight. It was clear to everyone that he was one of the best prospects in baseball.

Clear, that is, to everyone but Jimmy. That winter, he was looking at a magazine called *Sporting News,* and he read a story that said the Red Sox planned to ask him to go to Florida early and learn to play shortstop. Boston's new manager, Lou Boudreau, was quoted as saying that if Jimmy could handle playing shortstop, "I'll farm him out a year. I'd never take him as a shortstop right off."

The news sent Jimmy into a panic. This was the first he'd heard of playing shortstop. Instead of being flattered that the Red Sox thought he was good enough to change positions, he got the idea that they were trying to get rid of him, and he spent the rest of the winter deeply depressed. After telling his wife each day that he was going to the YMCA to work out, he hid in a movie theater, watching the same movie three or four times. When it came time to go to Florida, Jimmy was so certain that the Red Sox wanted to get rid of him that he had to be talked into going by his father and an old friend. Even then he decided to leave his glove behind. It didn't make much sense, but he convinced himself that if he left his glove at home, the Red Sox would be unable to make him play shortstop.

That's exactly how he felt when he arrived in Sarasota and took a cab to the team's hotel. And that was about the last thing he remembered of the 1952 baseball season. The treatment he underwent later made him forget almost everything that happened during the season.

Of course, when he got to Sarasota and the team found out he didn't have a glove, they had him borrow a glove from another player. Even though he was a nervous wreck over playing the new position, Jimmy learned quickly and impressed Lou Boudreau and Joe Cronin. In fact, despite what Boudreau had said earlier, on opening day in Washington, D.C., Jimmy was Boston's starting shortstop. President Harry Truman threw out the first pitch, and Jimmy played like a veteran, making no errors and hitting a double.

Then, ever so slowly, he started having trouble. In a game versus the Yankees he fielded a routine ground ball and threw it to first base. The throw pulled first baseman Billy Goodman's foot off the bag, but Goodman swiped at the runner with his glove as he ran past, trying to tag him. The umpire thought Goodman missed and called the runner safe.

From his position as shortstop, Jimmy thought the runner was out. He dashed across the field, arms waving, started screaming at the umpire, and was thrown out of the game. Although that kind of thing happens occasionally, it was unusual for a player—particularly a rookie—to run all the way across the field to argue about a routine play.

A few days later, as they warmed up before the game,

Jimmy and Yankee infielder Billy Martin began needling each other. Soon their words turned more serious and Martin motioned to Jimmy to meet him under the stands. The two got into a fistfight before other players broke them up. Jimmy ripped his shirt, so Lou Boudreau sent him to the clubhouse to change. His teammate, pitcher Mickey McDermott, tried to get Jimmy to cool down by joking with him, but that only made Jimmy madder, and he got into another fight, attacking McDermott. Boudreau then pulled him from the lineup. Jimmy tried to laugh it off, saying, "I might as well stop [fighting]. I haven't won one yet," but on the bench he was almost uncontrollable. All game long he screamed and yelled at Martin, ignoring his manager and teammates when they pleaded with him to stop.

Jimmy's own teammates began to realize that something was wrong, and most of them stayed out of his way. He started mocking some of them on the field, making fun of the way they ran. Boudreau, thinking Jimmy's behavior might be caused by the pressure he felt playing shortstop, moved him to right field. His behavior only became worse. When he went out to his position, he often took off his hat and bowed to the crowd, then did calisthenics. Boston fans loved his antics, which only led him to act out even more, clowning around during the games, making easy catches look difficult.

Jimmy fooled around on the bases, too. One time he reached first base off veteran pitcher and Negro League legend Satchel Paige. As Jimmy led off the base, he started imitating Paige, pantomiming his wind-up. Then he began flapping his arms like a chicken and oinking like a pig. It bothered Paige so much that he ended up walking the bases loaded, and giving up a grand slam to lose the game, but Jimmy's teammates still found his behavior embarrassing. On another occasion Jimmy started doing a hula dance on the field, and when a relief pitcher was transported from the bullpen by a jeep, Jimmy stuck out his thumb as if he were hitchhiking.

Although the crowd howled at Jimmy's hijinks and he was popular with fans, his manager and teammates reacted, as one reporter wrote, "with cold fury." Jimmy was beginning to act strangely on the bench and in the clubhouse, too, once breaking into tears when Boudreau told him at the last minute that he was not playing. From one night to the next, there was no telling what he might do, and he hardly had a friend on the team.

Finally, on June 28, despite the fact that Jimmy was hitting almost .300, the Red Sox ran out of patience. Boudreau called Piersall's attitude "detrimental to the club." General manager Joe Cronin added, "There really is a bad situation on the bench and in the clubhouse." They sent Jimmy down to their farm team in Birmingham, where he had played so well the previous year. They hoped he would settle down.

But at the Boston airport Jimmy spoke to a reporter and made insulting comments about his teammates and manager. Although he told his wife, "I am going to behave myself," and he hit a home run in his first at bat for Birmingham, before long he was acting even more strangely than before.

Once, when he was at bat, each time the pitcher began to wind up, Jimmy dropped his bat and imitated the wind-up, causing a long delay. Sometimes he would run from the batter's box to the third-base coach or back to the dugout after every pitch, as if he were receiving secret instructions. When it was time to go out on the field, he would stop to talk to the infielders on the way or race from the outfield back to the dugout for no apparent reason.

In one game, in probably his oddest performance, he chased after a ball as if he were a dog, getting down on all fours and pointing at it. Then he would kick the ball away and chase after it again. In only a few weeks he was thrown out of half a dozen games and suspended four times. He flew back to Boston twice, even though the team hadn't asked him to come.

On one flight he noticed the Boston sports reporter Ed Cunningham on the plane. Jimmy went over to him and spoke nonstop for the rest of the flight, his words pouring out in a stream. Some made sense and some didn't. Cunningham was disturbed by what he heard and the way Jimmy acted. A few days later he wrote, "It's my considered opinion that the less written now the better . . . a complete press blackout would be the best medicine that can possibly be described. I'm no authority on such matters, but my guess is he's heading straight for a nervous breakdown."

Soon the Red Sox came to the same conclusion. One morning a few days later they asked Jimmy to come to the ballpark for a meeting with general manager Cronin and several doctors. After talking with Jimmy for a few minutes, the doctors saw that he was clearly disturbed. They suggested that he take a rest and go to a private mental hospital, known as a sanitarium, for a few days to be evaluated. Jimmy didn't want to go, screaming and racing around the room and gesturing wildly, but after speaking with his wife, he reluctantly agreed.

Unfortunately, Jimmy got worse at the sanitarium. Each time the doctors tried to give him a shot of medication to help him calm down, he ran away. Then one day he lost complete control.

He refused the medication and started to fight, swinging wildly at the doctors and attendants, yelling and screaming the whole time. He became too violent to control, and the staff had to call the police. Because he had become violent, he was committed to a state mental hospital. Once he was there, the doctors released a brief statement that referred to him as "a very, very sick boy."

It was the best thing that could have happened to him. He wouldn't be able to run away and would finally get the treatment he so desperately needed.

The doctors diagnosed Jimmy with a mental illness that was then known as manic depression, which caused his mood to swing wildly between periods of high energy and excitability to deep depression. Today it is called bipolar disorder, but scientists are still uncertain exactly what causes the illness. Some believe it is caused by chemical imbalances in the brain and can be triggered by changes in a person's life. Or it might be inherited. In Jimmy's case, it seems likely that he had been suffering from a mild form of manic depression for years and it was set off when the Red Sox decided to have him switch positions.

Whatever the reason, it wasn't Jimmy's fault. Mental illness is *never* the patient's fault. Jimmy was mentally ill, just as a person can be physically sick with a physical illness such as pneumonia. Expecting him to recover without the help of doctors would be like expecting a cancer patient to get better without seeing a physician.

Now that doctors finally knew what was wrong with Jimmy, they set out trying to help him get better. At the time, there were only a few treatments for manic depression. One was psychotherapy, a series of intensive counseling sessions with a trained professional who can help a patient understand and control his or her behavior. Jimmy started counseling right away, but his doctor soon recommended another treatment. In what is known as electroshock therapy, a patient is given a highly controlled jolt of electricity to the brain. Although the treatment later became very controversial because it was sometimes dangerous and overused, for some patients it was also effective and is sometimes used even today.

Although scientists aren't quite sure why it works, electroshock therapy combined with psychotherapy helped Jimmy. After two weeks at the hospital he suddenly felt as if he "awoke." He found himself strapped to a bed, being told it was time to eat. He didn't know where he was or why. When he asked, an attendant told him he had been sick and was in a hospital.

Then Jimmy realized that something else was different. The headaches that had plagued him for years were gone.

Over the next few days he talked with his doctors and learned the extent of his illness. A byproduct of electroshock therapy was amnesia. Apart from the birth of his daughter in the spring, Jimmy remembered virtually nothing that had happened since he reported to Sarasota the previous January. He had no idea that he had played for the Red Sox, and he had no recollection of all his strange behaviors.

His doctor patiently explained his illness to Jimmy and told him that nothing he had done had been his fault. He was better now, and with help, there was no reason he could not remain well, resume his major-league career, and live a normal life.

Over the next few weeks Jimmy was stunned to learn from his wife that he had opened the season as the Red Sox shortstop and that they had been living in a Boston suburb. When he read the press clippings about the season in a scrapbook his father had maintained, Jimmy felt as if he were reading about a different person. He could not believe some of the things he had done. When teammates and neighbors came to visit him, he had no idea who they were.

Jimmy was deeply embarrassed and afraid of what people would think — whether they'd be afraid of him because they thought he was "crazy." But his doctor told him simply to tell people that because of his illness, he didn't remember what had happened. When Jimmy's story reached the newspapers, he began to receive hundreds and hundreds of letters of support from his fans. Many wrote to him that they had experienced the same or similar illnesses, and nearly everyone offered Jimmy their support. "They're all with me," said Jimmy of his fans after his illness. "How can I miss?"

The Red Sox were terrific to Jimmy. They assured him that if he remained healthy, there was still a spot on the team for him the next season, and when he was released from the hospital in August, they offered to send him and his family to Florida so he could continue his recovery. He agreed, and got into the best shape of his life. Now that he wasn't worrying all the time, he found life much, much easier. At spring training in 1953 his teammates welcomed him back and were happy to find him so relaxed and so positive.

About the only people not happy with Jimmy's recovery were the opposition. As Red Sox right fielder that season, Jimmy was terrific, making one sensational catch after another and hitting .272. As one sportswriter noted at the end of the season, "More than any other player the comeback big leaguer of 1953 is Jim Piersall, the twenty-three-year-old right fielder of the Boston Red Sox. He came back farther than any of them."

Jimmy Piersall went on to have a long, successful major-league career for Boston, the Cleveland Indians, the New York Mets, and the California Angels, even making the All-Star team for the Red Sox in 1954. Never shy about speaking out on his illness, in 1955 he told his story in a book called Fear Strikes Out, *which helped millions of people understand mental illness and led countless people to seek*

medical treatment. Jimmy had a few mild episodes of manic depression later in his life, but he continued to seek treatment as needed. After he retired from the game, he worked as a coach and a manager before having a long career as a broadcaster.

RON LeFLORE: PAROLED
TO PLAY BALL

ONE SUMMER DAY IN 1973, Michigan state prisoner number B115614 sat with a group of inmates watching television in a common area of a prison parole camp. Most of the men were longtime career criminals imprisoned for such crimes as robbery, assault, and drug dealing. As they neared the end of their sentences, the men had been sent to parole camp to prepare for life outside of prison. Most had already been in and out of prison many times, and many were destined to return.

On the television screen was the nationally broadcast major-league baseball *Game of the Week*. The contrast between the scene on the screen, where men ran free on a green field playing a game for a living, and the scene at the

camp, where men watched the seconds tick by in drab sur-
roundings, could not have been more dramatic.

One man, however, watched the action more closely
than the others. Ron LeFlore, prisoner B115614, studied the
screen intently. Imprisoned nearly four years earlier for
armed robbery, LeFlore had earned parole and in a few
weeks was scheduled to be released.

As the men sat watching, Ron suddenly spoke up.

"See those players?" he said, pointing toward the screen.
"Next year you guys are going to be watching a baseball
game on TV, and you're going to see me, because I'm going to be in the big leagues in one year's time."

A few prisoners turned their heads in Ron's direction.
Some laughed, and some simply shook their heads in dis-
belief. Oh, many of them knew Ron was a good ballplayer,
a star on the prison team, but the notion that someone
who had spent the last few years in prison would be playing major-league baseball the following summer was ludi-
crous. They knew he was far more likely to be back in
prison.

Even Ron didn't really believe what he had said, but
now that he had told others of his dream, he was more determined than ever to make it come true. He knew that so
far, he had done nothing but waste his life stealing and us-

ing drugs and getting into fights. When he walked out of prison in a few weeks, he was determined not to come back.

The only numbers he wanted to be known by were the numbers on the back of his uniform and on his baseball card.

Ron LeFlore was born and raised on the east side of Detroit, Michigan. His parents, John and Georgia, had moved to Detroit during World War II from Memphis, Tennessee. John got a job working at an auto factory, and soon the LeFlores had four sons, Marvin, Henry, Gerald, and Ron, the third oldest, who was born in 1950.

Ron's parents worked hard, were involved with his education, and saw to it that he went to church. But even so, he was difficult to control as a young boy. He took advantage of the fact that both his parents were working, and he often played hooky and hung out on the streets.

Detroit's east side was a tough neighborhood. Although most residents were hard-working, it was a poor community, and some people had drug problems. Ron's own father struggled with alcoholism. As a result, many people in the neighborhood didn't work for a living. They survived by dealing drugs, robbing people, stealing, and breaking the law. Ron later said, "The favorite pastime of the community was committing crimes."

Although Ron was smart and did well in school, even skipping a grade, he rarely went to school regularly. When he did, he was bored and found it hard to sit still. He got into fights and other trouble for such behavior as missing classes or cheating. He was often suspended and transferred, eventually attending nine different schools.

When Ron was hanging out on the streets, he always managed to find trouble. Since he saw people committing crimes and using drugs and alcohol all around him, he thought such activities were normal. He looked up to the older kids he saw and did what they did. When he went into a store, as he later wrote, "I would steal something, even if it was only a rubber ball . . . just to show the other kids I could do it." On the rare occasions when he got caught and his parents found out, he would usually be spanked, but that just made him more determined not to get caught. He lied to his parents regularly about how he was spending his time, and they had little idea just how badly he was behaving.

When Ron was twelve years old, he had a weekend job

cleaning up at a neighborhood grocery store, but instead of working hard, he stole from the store. Once, he walked out with a cart full of food. Several years later he stole $1,500 in cash from the same store, and then he tried to steal from the store again. This time he got caught and was placed on probation, which meant that if he got caught in another criminal act, he could go to jail.

By the age of nine Ron was smoking cigarettes. He began drinking alcohol at age eleven and doing drugs at thirteen. Despite the way he was abusing his body, he was one of the best athletes in his neighborhood. And although he liked sports, he wasn't serious about playing. He spent a few years playing in a church basketball league and sometimes played football or stickball on the streets. His father occasionally took him and his brothers to Tiger Stadium to see the Detroit Tigers play baseball, but as Ron later remembered, he "just wasn't interested." He didn't collect baseball cards or read about the games in the newspaper.

The only sport Ron ever thought about playing seriously was football. When he played on the streets, no one could catch him. He was sure he would be a star player someday. In high school he tried out for the team, but then he hurt his shoulder and had to quit. When that healed, he decided to play basketball, but he skipped school so often that he got kicked off the team. Finally, at age fifteen, after being caught and arrested for several small crimes, Ron quit school. He began spending much of his time at a neighborhood poolroom, hanging out. As he later wrote, "I noticed that most of the guys who hung out around the poolroom didn't work . . . and didn't seem to have a care in world. That was the life for me."

Once Ron stopped going to school, he had even more time to get into trouble, and it didn't take long for him to find it. He and four of his friends broke into a store and tried to crack open a safe, but they didn't know what they were doing, and they were caught. Since Ron was still on probation, he was sentenced to serve two to five years at the Michigan Training Unit.

Although in many ways MTU was more like a boarding school than a prison, discipline was strict, and Ron didn't like being told what to do and when to do it. He was forced to attend school during the day, and he was locked in his room each night. There were no girls to flirt with and very few opportunities to have fun. And Ron hated being locked up.

At first he was determined to turn his life around. He wanted to play football but knew he had to get good grades and behave in order to do so. He took his studies seriously and began to dream of earning a college football scholarship.

By this time, however, he was so accustomed to breaking the rules that he did so without even thinking about it. One day he saw a test for his biology class left out in the open. He stole the test and tried to sell it to his classmates. He was caught, kicked out of MTU, and sent across the street to the Michigan Reformatory.

The reformatory was a prison for teenage men. They all had to wear the same prison uniforms, they lived in cells, and they had very little freedom.

There were rules for *everything* — how to walk, when to eat, even when they were allowed to talk. Unfortunately for Ron, he still would not follow the rules, and he was often in trouble. Sometimes he was punished by being locked in his cell for days at a time. With each passing day he grew more angry and bitter. Any thoughts he had about turning his life around quickly faded away. When he was released after serving nineteen months, he resumed a life of crime.

He began working for drug dealers, serving as a lookout for the police, and he started using hard drugs on a regular basis. He never got a real job. When he needed money, he would steal something and sell it to the dealers in exchange for drugs, or he would rob a store with his friends. Sometimes one of his friends would distract a clerk while Ron robbed the cash register. Other times they would brazenly walk out with merchandise, threatening the owners with physical harm if they called the police.

One night in 1970, when Ron was nineteen years old, he was hanging out with two friends, Leroy and Antoine, when they ran out of money for drugs and decided to rob a bar. So far, despite all the crimes Ron had committed, he had never been involved in a crime with a gun. This time, however, he and his friends were worried that the bar owner might be armed. So they borrowed a rifle and waited until the bar was almost empty before bursting in through the back door.

Ron held the gun and aimed it at the owner. "This is a robbery," he called out. "Don't make any wrong moves, and nobody will get hurt!" Ron and his friends emptied the cash register, grabbed a bag of cash from an open safe, and fled in his friend's car.

But Ron and his friends were hardly master criminals. When driving away from the bar, they forgot to turn the car lights on and were spotted by the police. After they stashed the money at Leroy's apartment, Ron walked out of the building and found himself surrounded by the police.

Ron and his friends were arrested. Because Ron had been holding the gun, he faced the most serious charge—"assault with intent to commit robbery, armed." In exchange for a lighter sentence Leroy testified against Ron at the trial, and Ron was quickly found guilty.

The judge lectured him before he pronounced the sentence. He called him a "menace to society" and told him that since he had been carrying the gun and might have shot someone, he intended to sentence him to twenty to forty years in prison. Ron couldn't believe what he was hearing.

Then he got lucky. The judge had spoken to his parents. His mother had told him how intelligent Ron was, and the judge took pity on him. Instead of a sentence of twenty to forty years, he gave him a sentence of five to fifteen years.

The words barely registered. As far as Ron was concerned, five years or fifteen years didn't matter. He was going to prison, and this time he would be with men who were in prison for murder and other violent crimes.

A few days later he was transferred from the jail to begin his sentence. Along with other prisoners, Ron was handcuffed and put into a police station wagon with bars on the windows. When they got to Jackson State Prison, the largest walled prison in the world, home for more than six thousand prisoners, Ron was afraid. Of all the prisons in Michigan, Jackson State was the worst. It was a maximum security facility, designed to hold the most dangerous prisoners. The massive walls were covered with razor wire, and armed guards constantly patrolled the grounds, looking for escapees.

Ron was led inside, searched, and given his prison clothes. Then he was led to his cell, one of hundreds on five levels in the enormous prison.

He felt as if he would never get out.

Prisoners in a maximum security facility have very little control over their lives. Except for a small period of time when they are allowed to exercise in the yard or work at a job, prisoners spend most of their time in their cells, and they have to follow a very strict set of rules.

Ron did exactly as he was told, and within a few months he was fortunate enough to be transferred to a prison farm. During the day the prisoners tended the fields, raising crops and taking care of livestock, and at night they slept in barracks.

But Ron wasn't used to working. Within a few days he refused to do his job. He was sent back to Jackson and punished by being put into solitary confinement.

His cell was only a few square yards and his bed a steel cot with no mattress, no sheets, blanket, or pillow. He wasn't permitted a radio or reading material and was allowed out of his cell only once a week to shower. All he could do was spend his time daydreaming and exercising, doing push-ups and sit-ups and walking back and forth until he passed out from exhaustion.

It was horrible, but Ron wasn't ready to change. During his first year and a half in prison he kept on breaking the rules and being sent to solitary. As soon as he got out, he would be sent back in.

Ron finally realized that if he kept breaking the rules, he would never qualify for parole and leave prison early. Instead, he would probably serve out his entire term. By the time he got out, he would be thirty-five years old.

Ever so slowly, Ron began to change. Although he still occasionally bent prison rules, he managed to get a job in the kitchen as a cook. He was still a terrific athlete, and when he learned that prisoners who played on the prison baseball team often had a better chance at earning parole, he decided to try out for the team.

At that point in his life Ron had never, ever played baseball. In fact, he had never even hit a baseball with a real baseball bat. Yet he was such a strong natural athlete and such a fast runner that he made the team and earned a spot in the lineup as left fielder.

As a member of the team, Ron was allowed to spend more time in the prison yard. The team practiced every afternoon. On weekends local semipro and amateur teams came to the prison for games.

Ron rapidly improved, but he still didn't know how to play very well. He had never really watched and studied baseball. When he was at bat, he swung as hard as he could at almost every pitch. In the field he often misjudged fly balls, but he was able to make up for his mistakes with his speed and strong throwing arm. On the bases he didn't know how to take a lead off base or how to slide properly, but he was still so fast that he stole bases with ease.

An older prisoner named Jimmy Karella saw Ron play and thought he had real ability. Karella had helped coach sports in high school, and he soon began working with Ron, hitting him hundreds of extra fly balls and grounders and talking to him about the way the game was played.

After only a few months, Karella told Ron he had the ability to play professional baseball.

At first Ron didn't believe him, but Karella was insistent. Slowly, Ron began to believe that maybe he really did have a future in baseball. It was the first time he felt he was good at anything other than stealing and getting into trouble.

Ron wrote to the major-league Detroit Tigers and asked for a tryout when he got out of prison. The Tigers sent him back a form letter saying they weren't interested. But that didn't stop him. With each passing day he became more and more determined to play professional baseball.

He knew that in order to have a chance, he had to get out of prison, and in order to get out of prison, he had to change. For the first time in his life Ron had a goal.

He began to follow the prison rules, and he got involved in a number of programs, such as Narcotics Anonymous and Alcoholics Anonymous. He started going to church and attended group counseling sessions where prisoners discussed their lives and tried to understand why they ended up in prison. Ron and another prisoner even set up an athletic program for inmates with mental and emotional problems.

The better Ron played baseball, the better he behaved. After hitting .469 for the prison team in 1971, his first season, the following year he hit .569. He also earned the privilege of living in the prison's "honor block," a special section for the best-behaved inmates, who are allowed a few special privileges, such as additional time out of their cell.

Finally, in March 1973 Ron had his first hearing before the parole board, which looks at the inmate's record in prison and has the power to decide to allow him to leave early.

The board was impressed with Ron's turnaround, but they were also skeptical. After all, he had spent a total of five months in solitary confinement. They knew that some prisoners act as if they have changed in order to be released early, and they often return to crime shortly after leaving prison.

One member of the board asked Ron if he thought he deserved to be released. "Yes, I do," Ron said. Then he spoke honestly, telling the board that he realized he had made many mistakes and had continued to make mistakes when he first entered prison. He hoped the board would take into account the way he had become involved in various programs and learned to adhere to the rules.

The board didn't make a decision right away, but a few days later Ron learned that he had been granted parole. In ninety days, he would be leaving prison.

He was determined not to blow it. He later recalled, "As soon as I learned I was going to be released, I became obsessed with baseball, working harder than ever before." Then one of Jimmy Karella's friends, Jimmy Butsicaris, who was a friend of the Detroit Tigers manager, Billy Martin, arranged for Martin to visit the prison and meet with the inmates. He told Martin all about Ron, adding that he might have the ability to play pro ball. Martin met Ron, and even though he didn't get a chance to see him play, he told Ron to come see him after he was released: "Whenever you're in Tiger Stadium, come out and I'll give you a workout."

Ron later called the visit "one of the greatest days of my life." While awaiting parole, he was allowed to live outside the prison in a parole camp, which was where he was on the day he told the other inmates that in a year's time they would be watching him in the major leagues. After staying in the camp for a number of weeks, Ron was given a forty-eight-hour furlough, which meant he would be allowed to spend a weekend out of prison.

The old Ron LeFlore would have immediately gotten into trouble and probably been rearrested. But he was a different person now. He knew exactly what he wanted to do. Before leaving camp, he called Billy Martin at Tiger Stadium and reminded him of his promise. Martin was true to his word and told him to come to the ballpark the next morning.

Ron walked out of parole camp that afternoon a free

man for the first time in almost four years. After spending the night with his family, he went to Tiger Stadium the next day.

Few other major-league teams would have taken a chance on a prisoner, but the Tigers had discovered outfielder and pinch hitter Gates Brown in a prison in Ohio, and Brown had been a valuable member of the team and a model citizen. They were willing to take a chance on Ron.

Shortly after Ron arrived at the ballpark, Martin told him to take batting practice, then sat back with the other Tiger players and coaches to watch.

As Ron stood in the batter's box, he had never been so nervous — not when breaking into a building to steal money, not when pointing a gun during the robbery of the bar, and not even when he entered prison for the first time. He knew his entire future might depend on what happened during the next few minutes.

The Tigers' batting-practice pitcher wound up and threw. Ron swung with all his might.

Whiff! The bat swished through the strike zone, hitting only air as the pitch sailed past Ron. He had missed it completely.

Yet that first swing calmed his nerves. When the next pitch came over the plate, he kept his eye on the ball. A loud *crack!* echoed through the ballpark as Ron's bat made contact.

With each swing he grew more confident. He didn't miss another pitch. Soon he was driving the ball deep into the left-field stands. He overheard one of the players say, "He's hitting 'em up in the upper deck the way Willie hits them," comparing Ron's blasts to those of Tiger slugger Willie Horton. After hitting, Ron went to the outfield, where he shagged flies for a while. Then he went to the locker room to shower.

The Tigers were impressed. They asked Ron to attend another tryout at a nearby field the following weekend so their scouts could take another look at him.

Ron was again released on furlough and this time Ron was even more impressive. One Tiger scout called him a "lightning bolt . . . the kind of player you build a championship team around." At the end of the tryout the Tigers offered Ron a professional contract — as soon as he got out of prison.

The next few weeks went by in a blur, but on July 2, 1973, Ron walked out of the prison a free man. More important, he was determined to remain a free man. Instead of going out and celebrating, he had his father drive him directly to Tiger Stadium, where he signed a contract that included a $5,000 bonus. He was told to report to the Tigers' minor-league team in Clinton, Iowa. Ron was out of prison and officially a professional ballplayer, but he was still a long way from the major leagues.

It was a tough adjustment. At first his teammates and coaches didn't trust him, and Ron had to learn to stop thinking like a criminal. When he went into a store, he immediately started thinking how easy it would be to steal something. He had to train himself to stop thinking that way.

It was no easier on the field. He quickly realized that although he was talented, the other players were much more skilled than he was. After getting an infield hit his first time up, Ron went his next seventeen at bats without a hit.

Fortunately, he was a quick learner, and he ended the season hitting a respectable .277. The Tigers sent him to Florida for the winter to play in the Instructional League and gain more experience. He really began to learn the game, and at the start of the 1975 season he was sent to the Tigers' minor-league team in Lakeland, Florida. He tore up the league and in midseason was hitting .339. He told a reporter that he thought he deserved a promotion to the Tigers' Double-A team in Montgomery, Alabama, only two steps below the major leagues.

He soon got his wish—but he wasn't promoted to Montgomery. The Tigers sent him to their best minor-league team, their AAA farm club in Evansville, Indiana. He was one step short of the major leagues.

Ron was thrilled. He hardly believed that in only one year he had made it so far.

He had been with Evansville less than two weeks when the phone rang, waking him from a deep sleep. It was Evansville's general manager.

"You're going to Detroit," he said.

Ron, half awake, couldn't believe what he was hearing. "What for?" he asked.

"To play center field," answered the general manager.

Ron packed quickly and met the team on the road in Milwaukee. The regular center fielder, Mickey Stanley, had broken his hand. The manager, Ralph Houk, who had taken over after Billy Martin was fired, told Ron, "You're starting tonight. You're going to be my center fielder."

In his first game, Ron had a rough start, striking out

three times. But in his second game he got a base hit and stole two bases. Then the Tigers flew back to Detroit to open a home stand.

Ron was thrilled to have the opportunity to play before his hometown fans. He could hardly believe he was standing on the same field with such players as slugger Willie Horton and all-time great Al Kaline. His parents were in the stands, and his brother and a bunch of old friends from the neighborhood were all sitting together in center field and waving a banner with Ron's name on it.

Just before the start of the game, Ron was called onto the field to give a television interview. The game was featured on the nationally televised *Game of the Week*, the same series he had watched from parole camp more than a year earlier, when he boasted to other inmates that in another year they would be watching him on television.

When the interview ended, Ron ran out to center field. Instead of the harsh cries of convicts, he heard the cheers of the crowd. He was no longer prisoner number B115614, but number 8, the center fielder of the Detroit Tigers. He had turned his life around, and now there was no turning back.

Ron LeFlore went on to play nine seasons in the major leagues for the Tigers, the Montreal Expos, and the Chicago White Sox before retiring with a career batting average of .288. In 1976 he made the American League All-Star team, and he twice led his league in stolen bases, including ninety-seven stolen bases in 1980. After retirement Ron worked for an airline, attended umpire school, and coached. Although he has since struggled with some financial difficulties, he has been able to stay out of serious trouble and has never returned to the life of crime that once sent him to prison.

JOE TORRE'S BIGGEST VICTORY

AFTER THE FIRST GAME OF the 1996 World Series, George Steinbrenner, the impatient owner of the New York Yankees, was angry at the Yankees manager, Joe Torre. In his first year as New York's manager, Torre had taken his team to the World Series, where they faced the Atlanta Braves. But in game one, the Yankees had been blown out, losing 12–1. And now, ninety minutes before game two, Steinbrenner stormed into Torre's office at Yankee Stadium and told him bluntly, "This is a must game." He felt that if the Yankees lost game two to the Braves' ace pitcher Greg Maddux, it would be impossible for New York to come back and win the series. And sportswriters were already speculating that if the Yankees lost the series, Steinbrenner would fire Torre.

The Yankees owner was thinking the same thing. That's why he stormed into his manager's office.

Another manager might have panicked and made a rash decision, changing his lineup or his batting order. But that wasn't Joe Torre's style. He believed in his players, and even more important, he had recently learned to believe in himself. Torre remained at his desk and listened to Steinbrenner vent his dissatisfaction. Then he calmly spoke, barely glancing at his boss.

"Atlanta's my town," Torre said, in reference to the fact that he had once been the manager of the Braves. "We'll take three games there and win it back here [in New York] on Saturday."

Steinbrenner was taken aback. Torre was saying that he expected the Yankees to lose game two, then go on the road, beat the Braves three straight games in Atlanta, and come back to New York and win the series. The stunned owner could hardly believe his ears, and he stormed out of Torre's office.

But Joe Torre knew what he was talking about. He remained confident that his team, which had won ninety-two games during the regular season, was better than the

Braves. After all, Joe Torre and the Yankees had been coming from behind and overcoming problems all year long.

When Torre was hired in the off-season, few people thought he was the right man for the job. One New York headline called him "Clueless Joe." When the Yankees had gotten off slowly at the start of the season, it seemed as if the critics were correct. But Joe believed in his players, and the Yankees had overcome their slow start to win the American League's Eastern Division title. Then, even though they had fallen behind in the American League Division Series to the Texas Rangers, and then to the Baltimore Orioles in the American League Championship Series — with Torre's steady leadership the Yankees had come back to win each time.

It had not been easy for Torre. His oldest brother Rocco had passed away in midseason, and his other older brother, Frank, was critically ill with a heart condition, awaiting a heart transplant. Yet Torre managed to remain calm and focused and set an example for his players. No matter what happened or whatever misfortune his team faced, Joe Torre stayed the same. He never panicked, but exuded a quiet confidence that seemed to give his players the confidence they needed to play their very best when it mattered most.

To baseball fans, it seemed as if Joe Torre had been born

with ice water in his veins. Very few of them, however, knew the truth. Growing up in Brooklyn as a boy and young man, he had been anything but confident. In fact, he had been so insecure and so afraid that he thought he might never succeed at anything.

Pudgy little Joe Torre, age ten, was frozen with fear.

From the outside, the brick row house at 3322 Avenue T looked no different from the other homes on the quiet Brooklyn street. Flowers hung from pots on the porch, and the grass and bushes were neat and trim.

Inside the house, however, Joe was terrified. He was only a kid, but instead of looking forward to each day, he sometimes dreaded waking up. He never knew what mood his father might be in.

A detective for the New York City Police Department, Joseph Torre was known to other police officers as "the Boss" owing to his gruff, no-nonsense demeanor. They respected and looked up to him. Unfortunately, the toughness that served him so well on the police force did not lead to a happy home for Joe, his two brothers, his two older sisters, and his mother.

Detective Torre usually worked the late shift and rarely came home before two or three in the morning, then slept until the following afternoon. Joe and the other Torre children had to stay quiet and try to keep from waking their father. They were even more afraid when he was awake, because from one moment to the next, Joe's father, for little reason, could explode with anger. When he became angry, he also became violent, sometimes striking his wife and children or screaming at them and threatening them with harm.

Almost every day, little Joe awoke with his stomach in knots, afraid of what his father might do. He tried to stay out of his father's way and sought comfort in his mother's Italian cooking, stuffing his face to make up for some of the emptiness and pain he felt. His two older brothers, Rocco and Frank, were tremendous athletes, and Frank had become a professional baseball player. Joe loved baseball too, but he was nearly as wide as he was tall. He didn't look as if he'd ever be a high school player, much less a professional. Even his brothers teased him about his weight, which only made him eat more.

One day Joe's father got into an argument with Joe's teenage sister Rae over some small issue. Rae, afraid her father might hit her, grabbed a kitchen knife and waved it in front of her in self-defense.

This made her father angrier. His face beet red, he screamed at his daughter to put the knife down, and she backed off, crying and shaking.

A few steps away, little Joe watched the confrontation, not certain what would happen next. He saw his father turn and reach toward a drawer in the dining room. Joe knew that was where his father kept his police gun when he was off duty. If his father got his gun, Joe was afraid he just might use it.

Rae was paralyzed, holding the knife before her, staring at her father. Joe suddenly rushed to his sister's side, grabbed the knife from her hand, and called to his father. "Here!" he said, and placed the knife on the table.

His father stopped in his tracks and spun around. Then he spied the knife on the table, picked it up, turned around, and put it away. As quickly as the argument started, it had stopped, and the house was suddenly quiet.

Joe knew that the quiet was only temporary. Although there were times when his father laughed and was full of life, Joe felt as if it was impossible to relax whenever he was around. He loved his father, but at the same time he hated the way he treated his brothers and sisters and mother, and he hated the way it made him feel. He was, as he wrote later, "a nervous, self-conscious kid without an ounce of self-confidence."

Joe was the youngest in the family, and there was little he could do to make the situation better. But a year later, after his sister Marguerite moved out of the house to become a nun, leaving Joe, his sister Rae, and his mother at home alone with his father, things continued to deteriorate. Whenever his father got into another confrontation and beat his wife, Joe's mom would call Frank — who was away playing baseball — for comfort. That year, the calls to Frank became more and more frequent. When Frank returned to Brooklyn at the end of the season, he told his mother that it was time to ask his father to leave, that it would be better for everyone in the family. Joe's mom agreed.

Little Joe, Frank, his mother, and his sister were all sitting at the kitchen table one evening when Frank asked his father to come in. His father sat down, and Frank bluntly told him that no one in the family wanted him to stay and that he had to leave the house and never come back. Joe's father wasn't happy, but Frank was a grown man and too big to be intimidated. Joe's father moved out and eventually divorced his mother.

For young Joe Torre it was as if a great cloud had lifted. He no longer had to worry about what might happen at home. Although part of him missed his father, he also knew that he no longer had to fear that his father would beat his mother or his sister.

Although Joe felt somewhat better, there were still feelings and effects that would take him years to overcome. A few years after his father left, Joe's brother Frank made it to the major leagues with the Milwaukee Braves. Joe wanted to play baseball as well, but even though things were better at home without his father, he still lacked confidence, later calling himself "the champion of self-defeat." He didn't get involved in any high school activities or go on dates, and he didn't even make his high school team until he was a junior. Playing third base, first base, and pitcher, he did well, hitting over .500 as a senior, and for the first time in his life he began to gain a little confidence. Unfortunately, he was still overweight, and major-league scouts were not interested. After graduating from high school, he got a job at the American Stock Exchange and prepared for a life without baseball.

But he couldn't give up on the game. That summer, he played on an amateur team known as the Cadets, and Frank Torre convinced the manager to have Joe play catcher. His size wasn't as much of an impediment behind the plate, and with all the extra exercise he got crouching down after every pitch, Joe began to lose weight. When the team played in a national tournament later that summer, baseball scouts who had previously ignored him began to pay attention, and the Milwaukee Braves, Frank's team, soon offered him a contract to play professional baseball.

Joe went on to have a fine major-league career, playing for eighteen years with the Braves, the St. Louis Cardinals, and the New York Mets. He made the All-Star team nine times, won the batting title, and was named National League Most Valuable Player in 1971 with the Cardinals, hitting .363 and leading the league in hits and runs batted in.

But Joe's career was not a total success. None of his teams ever made it to the playoffs or the World Series, and off the field he had a tough time. He continued to struggle with his weight for much of his career, had difficulty balancing his baseball career with his home life, and was married and divorced twice, writing later that even as an adult, "home was never a comfortable place" for him. Owing to his experiences as a young boy with his father, he didn't feel that he was as good a husband and father as he wanted to be. Although he wasn't violent like his father, he was so accustomed to keeping his feelings inside that he had a hard time relating to his own wife and children.

It wasn't until he became a baseball manager that Joe really began to change. Even then, it was a long process.

His first managerial job was with the New York Mets, from 1977 through 1981. The Mets weren't a very good team, and Joe wasn't a very good manager. Many of his team members still knew him from his playing days, and he had a rough time gaining their respect. Although the players liked him, they simply didn't perform well for him, and they sometimes took advantage of his laid-back personality, compiling a record of 286–420 in five seasons. After he was fired by the Mets, Joe took over as manager of the Atlanta Braves for three years. Then, after being a broadcaster for six years, he managed the St. Louis Cardinals for six seasons before being fired in early 1995. Although both teams performed better than the Mets, Joe took his team to the playoffs only once.

At age fifty-four, after leaving the Cardinals, Joe went to work as a broadcaster again. He had married for the third time, and his wife, Ali, was expecting a baby. Joe figured his career as a big-league manager was over.

Then the unexpected happened. Soon after the Yankees were defeated in the 1995 playoffs, the Yankee manager

Buck Showalter resigned. Joe was shocked when the Yankees asked him to be their next manager.

Even though it meant working with George Steinbrenner, the team's demanding owner, Joe accepted the job. The Yankees were already one of the best teams in baseball, and he knew that if he didn't take them to the World Series — and win it — he would probably be fired. He figured he had nothing to lose.

Just a few weeks before spring training, Joe's wife asked him to attend a meeting at a hotel about how to become a better person, sort of a "self-help" course. She realized that he had a hard time expressing his feelings when they talked, and she thought the course might help him. Joe wasn't really interested, but he agreed to go.

At the seminar, people were split into groups and were asked to talk about their past. When Joe heard other people talking about their childhood, he did as well, speaking publicly for the first time about how his father behaved and how he felt it affected him as a boy and a young man.

Even he was surprised by some of the things he said. By speaking out loud about his problems, he was admitting them to himself for the very first time. He began to realize that he had grown up in an abusive home and that it had affected him as an adult, making it difficult for him to express his emotions. Although he had never been violent, whenever there was trouble, instead of confronting it and talking about it, Joe withdrew and stayed quiet, which allowed small problems to become bigger problems. He realized that he had to be more open, not just to his wife but to everyone else, including his players.

Joe studied the issue, took a critical look at himself, and began to open up to his wife, family, and friends. By the time spring training began, he had never been more confident. He realized that his newfound perspective made him feel much more certain of his decisions as a manager. In the past, he would second-guess his decisions and wonder if he had done the right thing—all feelings left over from when he crept around the house hoping not to upset his father. Now he knew that he did not have to worry so much about what others felt. He could be himself, trust his decisions, and talk about them with his players.

The Yankees were already a playoff-quality team, full of such talented players as third baseman and eventual Hall of Famer Wade Boggs, center fielder Bernie Williams, slugger Darryl Strawberry, and star pitchers Andy Pettitte and David Cone, as well as talented rookie shortstop Derek Jeter and relief pitcher Mariano Rivera. Joe knew the Yankees had the talent to win.

Their previous manager, Buck Showalter, had been strict and harsh, much like owner George Steinbrenner. Showalter was very thorough, and he micromanaged every aspect of his team. Yet for all their talent, they often played tight and nervous baseball, playing more as if they were afraid to lose than simply trying to win.

Joe Torre took a different approach. He trusted his men to play the game the right way from the start. Some people thought the Yankees would benefit from his approach, while others thought the veteran team would walk all over Torre.

His hiring was controversial. After all, in fifteen seasons of managing and eighteen as a player, no Joe Torre team had *ever* made it to the World Series. Joe knew that the only way to prove them wrong was to win.

He decided to trust his players, and he knew that in order to do so, he had to be honest with them. If Joe believed that a certain player, for instance, was better hitting at the bottom of the order than at the top, he told him and told him the reasons why rather than just taking an action without explanation.

On one occasion early in the season, two Yankee outfielders miscommunicated, and a routine fly ball dropped between them for a hit. When Joe pulled the outfielder

from the game the next day, a Yankees broadcaster specu-
lated that it was because of the incident the day before.

It was not, and if it had been, Joe would have told the
player. When he saw the broadcaster in the clubhouse the
following day, Joe confronted him.

"I don't appreciate you trying to stir something up," he
said. "We've got a pretty good chemistry here." The Yankees players were impressed with the way their new manager handled the situation and stood up for his players,
and they began to respond to Joe's approach.

A ball club that many considered simply a collection of
superstars became a team. By the time the Yankees reached
the World Series, Joe had earned the trust and respect of
his players. Still, he knew that if the Yankees didn't win the
series, he would probably be fired.

After they lost the first game, George Steinbrenner had
made that pretty clear. And when the Yankees, as Torre
feared, lost not only game one to the Braves but game two,
4–0, to fall behind two games to none, the pressure was on
Joe to fulfill his prediction.

Under such pressure, the old Joe Torre, the pudgy young
boy who lived in fear, would have been nervous and afraid.
But over the years, culminating in the self-help course, Joe
had changed. He had opened up, and as he found it much

easier to talk with his wife and other members of his family, including his two older brothers, and to let them know how much he really cared about them, he realized just how much living in fear for so long had hurt his self-confidence. Now that he understood these things, he was able to leave those feelings behind.

For the remainder of the World Series, the new Joe Torre would be put to the test.

In game three, Torre selected David Cone to pitch, and in the sixth inning, with the Yankees clinging to a 1–0 lead, Cone was in trouble. He loaded the bases with one out and the Braves cleanup hitter, Fred McGriff, was coming to bat.

Joe knew it was a critical moment in the game. If the Braves got a hit, they would break the game wide open. The old Joe Torre might have made a pitching change, but now he went out to talk to his pitcher. He looked Cone in the eye and said, "I need the truth from you. How do you feel?" trusting his pitcher to tell him.

"I'm okay," said Cone. "I'll get this guy for you."

Joe left him in the game. He knew that if he was wrong, the Yankees would probably lose and he would be fired. But now he not only believed in himself, he believed in his players.

Cone got McGriff on a pop out and escaped the inning

giving up only a single run. The Yankees then went on to win the game 5–3. The next night, in game four, the Yankees fell far behind, 6–0, but under Joe Torre's leadership they never gave up. He told them not to try to score six runs at once but "take small bites. Do the little things to get one run at a time." If the Yankees did that, he knew the Braves would begin to feel the pressure.

That's exactly what happened. Torre didn't panic, and neither did his players. The Yankees chipped away, tied the score, and then won, 8–6, in extra innings. After beating the Braves 1–0 in game five behind Andy Pettitte, the Yankees returned to New York with a chance to win the World Series in game six, just as Torre had predicted.

But just after Joe arrived in New York, he received a phone call. His brother Frank had needed a heart transplant, and a donor had become available. He was already being prepared for surgery.

Fortunately, both teams had the day off. Joe was concerned, but over the past year he had finally been able to tell his brother how much he cared for him. He knew that even if Frank did not survive, he would be at peace because he had been able to tell him how he felt about him.

Later that day the phone rang again. It was Frank. He

had survived the surgery and was going to be okay. Even though Joe hardly slept owing to his concern for his brother, he was ready for game six.

One more time, he put his faith in his players. The Yankees jumped out to a 3–0 lead off Braves pitcher Greg Maddux, and they led 3–1 entering the ninth inning, when Torre turned to closer John Wetteland.

Wetteland had been terrific all year, although there were times when he made the games close. Yet Joe Torre had never lost faith in him.

This time he believed in him one more time. Despite the fact that Wetteland had given up three hits and a run, Torre left him in the game, not even rising from his seat to go talk with him. Wetteland then got Mark Lemke to hit a pop-up—to win the game and make the Yankees world champions.

Joe Torre finally had his World Series victory. But as his players sprayed him with champagne after the game, he knew that along the way, he had won something much more important.

"Clueless Joe" knew exactly who he was. He had defeated his own past.

Joe Torre went on to manage the Yankees through the 2007 season, winning three more world championships and taking his team into postseason play eleven times before becoming manager of the Los Angeles Dodgers. He also started his own foundation, the Joe Torre Safe at Home Foundation (www.joetorre.org), to provide help for children growing up in abusive homes.

TORII HUNTER: OVERCOMING EVERY OBSTACLE

THERE'S JUST SOMETHING ABOUT TORII HUNTER and fences.

Soon after becoming a regular player in 1999, Torii Hunter has been one of the best outfielders in the majors, known as much for his glove as his bat. Major-league baseball fans have become accustomed to the sight of Hunter hitting long home runs or dashing around the bases after hitting a line drive off the wall in the gap, making doubles from singles and triples from doubles. In the outfield they are no longer surprised to see Torii running back on a deep fly ball, then leaping at the last second, crashing into the fence, reaching his glove above the wall, and somehow catching the ball, turning certain home runs into outs, making catches that seem impossible.

What many fans don't realize is that the most amazing part of his life is not what he has done on the field, but what he has done off the field to make his career possible. Given the environment in which he grew up in Pine Bluff, Arkansas, a career in major-league baseball for Torii Hunter seemed absolutely impossible. The most amazing thing about him is not the way he plays on the baseball field, but the way he has overcome many obstacles to become a positive and responsible person. That's what makes him *really* special.

Pine Bluff is a small city of about fifty-five thousand people. Although many residents work hard, it is also a very poor community, with few opportunities for young people to get ahead. As a result, when Torii was growing up, many young people joined gangs and turned to crime and drugs. One magazine named Pine Bluff one of the ten "most impoverished cities in America," with nearly fifty percent of its residents considered poor. Another rated Pine Bluff as the very worst place in America to grow up.

Torii Hunter was born in Pine Bluff in 1975. His parents, Shirley and Theotis, were hard-working. Shirley was a teacher, and Theotis worked as an electrician for a local railroad. Still, with four children — Torii and his older brother, Taru, and younger brothers Tishque and Tramar — money was tight. Yet when Torii was a young boy, life was good. With brothers to play with and both parents usually working and involved in their lives, the Hunters were more fortunate than many other families in the neighborhood. Although there was little money to spare, they had most of what they needed. Besides, Torii was too young to realize that he lived in a dangerous place. It was just home.

The Hunters lived in a tough neighborhood. Many of the boys and young men in Pine Bluff belonged to gangs, and it was dangerous for the Hunter boys to be on the street. The gangs had divided up the city, and if a member of one gang was spotted on the "turf" of another, he could be beaten or even killed. The various gangs often sold drugs, stole cars, and committed other crimes. Even if a young man was not in a gang, he was still in danger of being mistaken for someone who was. Kids in Torii's neighborhood learned to look over their shoulder anytime they were on the street. Shootings and murders were so common that some residents called their town "Pine Box," like a coffin.

When Torii was growing up, an epidemic of crack co-caine use swept the country. Almost overnight, the drug ravaged communities everywhere. Many people who had never had drug problems before became addicts who were willing to do anything to get money to get more drugs. Drug dealers were commonplace, and in Torii's neighbor-hood many young men and women saw drug dealing as a way to become wealthy without working hard or going to school.

Unfortunately, as the boys grew older, Torii's family sit-uation began to change. His mother had to drive a long way to her teaching job, and his father was often away as well. The boys spent a lot of time unsupervised and had to grow up quickly and learn to take care of one another. By the age of ten Torii was doing most of the cooking for his brothers. They didn't mind, because Torii loved baking cakes more than preparing healthy, balanced meals.

But as soon as the boys left their house, they entered a different world. Taru, as the oldest, began to spend time on the streets, and he joined a gang, as much for self-protec-tion as anything else. He simply didn't feel safe on the streets unless he was in a gang. He knew it was wrong, but it was hard to resist.

Taru knew that Torii idolized him and looked up to him as a father figure. He was determined to protect Torii from the worst part of life on the street, and he told other gang members to leave his brother alone. He knew that gang life was dangerous and didn't want his brother to become a part of it.

All the Hunter boys were fine athletes. When Torii was young, he and Taru played catch with a baseball or a football any chance they could get. Taru would throw the ball as far and high as he could and challenge Torii to catch it. The boys spent hours playing.

For Torii, playing sports became a way to stay out of trouble and stay safe. Torii's mother, in particular, encouraged all her children to play sports. She knew that the more she kept them busy, the less time they would have to get into trouble. All her sons played every sport available to them: baseball in the spring and early summer, track and football in the fall, and basketball in the winter. When the boys were between sports activities, she tried to organize pickup games with other neighborhood kids.

Torii's first love was football. With his strong arm and speed, he played quarterback on offense and safety on defense. In baseball, he started playing T-ball at age eight.

It was, however, impossible for the boys to play sports twenty-four hours a day. As they grew older, it was also impossible for Shirley and Theotis to keep watch over their children. Then Theotis began to have problems of his own.

Torii didn't realize it at first, but his father began using crack cocaine. Although Theotis was bright and fun to be around, he was also troubled. A veteran of the war in Vietnam, he had started using drugs in Vietnam and periodically struggled with drug abuse. He would disappear for days at a time, he worked only occasionally, and he spent whatever money came into the house on drugs. There were times when the Hunters could not pay their bills. Bill collectors would come to the house, and the boys would hide in the back and pretend no one was home. Sometimes the electricity would be turned off because the bill hadn't been paid. Sometimes there was so little to eat in the house that Torii and his brothers would have ketchup sandwiches for supper or knock on the door of neighbors and ask for something to eat.

Torii was in ninth grade when he realized just how far his father had fallen. Theotis had been gone for days and so had Torii's favorite Chicago Bulls jacket. Then one morning he awoke to find that his father — and his jacket —

had returned. "I see it laying in the house and my dad sleeping on the couch," he told a reporter years later. "I knew he must have taken it. So I grabbed it and wore it to school."

Later that day, Torii raised his hand to answer a question in class and heard something fall onto the floor. He looked down and saw that it was a glass pipe used to smoke crack cocaine.

Torii was terrified. If a student at his school was found with a crack pipe or something like that, he or she would be kicked out for the rest of the year.

Torii thought fast. He scooped up the pipe, then raised his hand and asked if he could go to the bathroom. His teacher gave him permission, and by the time Torii got to the bathroom, he was crying and shaking with fear and concern for his father. He hid the pipe in the back of the toilet. Torii realized that his family was in terrible trouble.

It was an awful way for a young man to live, and it made street life look very attractive. Every day, Torii and his brothers saw drug dealers driving new cars and wearing fine clothes. Torii had to avoid that kind of temptation each day. Yet after seeing what drugs had done to his father, Torii never used drugs himself. Although many of his friends smoked marijuana and used other drugs, when they started to use them around Torii, he would tell them to put the drugs away or he would leave.

There were, however, some aspects of street life that Torii didn't avoid. It was dangerous on the street, and as Torii said later, "Everyone I knew had a gun, and so did I." Although he had a gun only for his own protection and wasn't a member of a gang, he often hung out with gang members and nearly became a victim of gang life.

There was violence everywhere, and even if he wasn't in a gang, Torii knew that his life could end at any time. "My whole life," he said, "my goal was not to get shot and killed." He had at least ten young friends who were eventually murdered and he narrowly averted being shot himself.

"I've seen bullets ring out, whiz right past me," he later recalled. His brother's car was once shot full of holes, and Torii admits that he once shot his gun in self-defense. On another occasion some gang members thought Torii and one of his friends had shot a young man named Chucky. They came looking for Torii.

He was with some opposing gang members, and when the two groups spotted each other, they squared off. Torii and his friends stood on one side, and the other gang gathered only a few steps away.

Almost everybody had a gun. Several members of each group already had their guns out, ready to fight. It was a life-or-death situation. If anyone pulled the trigger, members of each gang were certain to be shot and probably killed. Torii knew he was a target.

The situation was tense, and for a few minutes the two sides hurled insults back and forth, trash talking and taunting the other, hoping to start a fight. Fortunately, no one pulled the trigger. The groups went their separate ways. Torii was lucky to be alive, and he knew it.

He also knew that gang life would get him nowhere, and as he grew older, he turned more and more to sports and looked to sports for his future. That meant remaining drug free.

He began to see sports as his pathway out of a bad situation. "I put pressure on myself," he said later. "I needed to make it just for my family . . . [my father] was the reason. I thought, *if I make it, I'm going to have the money I need to get him help.*"

By the time Torii reached Pine Bluff High School, it was clear that he was one of the best athletes at the school. At first he thought his future was in football or basketball, where he was an immediate star as a sophomore for the Pine Bluff Zebras. Baseball was a bit more difficult for him.

Still, he soon got the attention of local baseball scouts. An older teammate, Basil Shabazz, was one of the best high school baseball players in the country. Scouts flocked to Pine Bluff games to see Shabazz play, and eventually he was drafted by the St. Louis Cardinals. But scouts who came to Pine Bluff to see Shabazz couldn't help but notice Torii.

Although he was young and skinny, he ran down fly balls with ease and had a strong arm and a quick bat. He was the kind of player scouts could look at and see that in a few years, once he got stronger and more mature, he would be a five-tool player—someone who could run, field, throw, hit, and hit with power. Players like that are rare and very valuable to a team.

Torii also had one more quality that the scouts loved—he wasn't satisfied with being just good. He wanted to be great. They watched how hard he worked at getting better and overcoming his circumstances. He was determined not to allow his background and upbringing to hold him back.

As a junior and a senior in high school, he earned all-state honors in baseball, and in 1992 he was named to the South squad for the U.S. Junior Olympic baseball team. He was honored by the selection, but in order to play on the team, he had to pay his own expenses to the tournament in South Korea — $1,200. For Torii, that might as well have been $12 million.

That didn't stop him. He sat down and wrote a letter explaining his situation to a number of prominent Arkansas residents, including Arkansas governor Bill Clinton, who later became president of the United States. Clinton was among a number of people who responded by sending Torii a check, and he was able to go to Korea.

But Torii still wasn't perfect. As a star athlete and a good-looking young man, he never had trouble getting a date, and before he graduated from high school, he had a child — a son — with one of his high school girlfriends. After seeing the way his own father abandoned his responsibilities, Torii was determined not to make the same mistake. He promised himself that he would take care of his son, and it gave him more motivation to make it as an athlete.

At the end of his senior year a number of colleges indicated that they were interested in offering him a scholarship to play baseball. Torii was interested, but then he heard rumors that he might be a first-round pick in the annual baseball draft. He knew that if he was drafted in the first round, it would be hard to turn down a contract.

More than fifty friends and family members gathered at the Hunter household on draft day, June 3, 1993, to learn which team had selected Torii. Although he hoped to be picked by the Atlanta Braves, his favorite team, when the phone rang, he learned that he had been selected by the Minnesota Twins with the twentieth pick in the first round of the draft.

Torii was overjoyed. As a first-round pick, he would have enough money to help take care of his family. A few days later the Twins' scouting director Mike Ruth came to Torii's house, and Torii signed a contract worth $450,000, more money than he had ever dreamed of earning. Against all odds, it seemed as if he would be able to escape the streets of Pine Bluff and help his family.

Most young men from Torii's situation would have blown the big bonus, spending the money on cars, clothes, and partying. Not Torii. Although he bought a few things for himself, he was determined to fulfill his responsibilities to his family and son. Most of the money went into the bank.

Although Torii was now a professional baseball player,

he did not have it easy. He struggled in his first season, hitting only .190 in the Gulf Coast League. But in his second year he began to show the Twins what he could do, hitting .293, with ten home runs, for Fort Wayne in the Midwest League. Yet he was still a long way from escaping the dangers of Pine Bluff.

Shortly after he returned home at the end of the 1995 season, his father took Torii's car and failed to come home. Torii spent five days looking for his father before he found his car parked outside a crack house. He went in and found his father passed out on the floor.

Torii lost his temper and beat up the other men in the house. Then he retrieved his car and took his father home. Later that night Torii and his old high school teammate Basil Shabazz, now a minor-league ballplayer himself, went to visit Torii's cousin at a nearby college. While Torii visited, Shabazz fell asleep in the car. Campus police knocked on the window to see if he was okay, and Shabazz, thinking he was being robbed, pulled a gun. Shabazz was arrested, and the police found Torii in the dormitory. They asked to search the car. Torii agreed. Then the police discovered marijuana and a crack pipe. Torii spent the night in jail.

The drugs and pipe belonged to Torii's dad, who had

left them in the car. Fortunately, both the police and the Twins believed Torii. Had they not, his baseball career could have come to a quick end. The incident made him realize that he had to be extra careful how he lived his life and who he hung out with. No one would believe him if something similar ever happened again. He did not want to destroy his chance — and that of his family — for a better life by making a stupid mistake.

For the next few seasons Torii made slow but steady progress, on the field and off. After having another child with a girlfriend, he settled down and married Katrina, whom he had known since high school. "I had a son in high school, and I had a son after high school, and that forced me to grow up," Torii later said. "I said, 'I can't be doing that . . . '" He wanted to be a better man and father as well as a good baseball player, and he was making progress on both fronts.

Most baseball fans became aware of Torii Hunter in the summer of 1997, when he was playing with New Britain in the Eastern League. Another player hit a long drive to the outfield, and Torii raced after the ball. As he neared the fence, he reached out his glove to make the catch, knowing he would probably strike the wall.

Just as he reached the fence, running at full speed, he caught the ball. He had no time to brace himself, and he hit the fence running as fast as he could.

But instead of hitting the wall and bouncing back onto the field, he went right through the wall! The old wooden fence gave way, and Torii seemed to disappear before running back through the fence a few moments later with the ball in his hand. A film of the catch was shown on sports programs all over the country.

A few months later Torii heard the word that every minor-league ballplayer hopes to hear. The Twins called and told him to report to Baltimore, where they were playing the Orioles. The Twins had made a trade and were temporarily short of players.

Torii knew he would probably spend only a few days in the major leagues, and he might not even get to play, but he found it hard to contain his excitement. Not only was he in the big leagues himself, but he would have a chance to see a major-league game for the first time. Growing up in Pine Bluff, he had never had that opportunity.

The date was August 22, 1997. Torii sat on the bench for most of the game, taking it all in and trying not to be nervous. He could hardly believe he was sitting on the same bench as Paul Molitor, the Twins star designated hitter who would later be elected to the Hall of Fame, or watching all-time great Cal Ripken play third base for the Orioles. Everything about life in the big leagues was impressive—the team hotel, the clubhouse, everything.

Torii tried to soak it all in. Then, in the ninth inning, manager Tom Kelly barked out his name and sent him in to pinch run for catcher Terry Steinbach who was on first base.

Torii waited until the umpire called time, then jogged out to first base, trying to act nonchalant. When he got there, he turned to Steinbach and said, "I'm supposed to run for you."

The veteran major leaguer just looked at him. "No, you're not," he said.

Torii froze. He wondered if he had misheard his manager and made a big mistake. Steinbach saw the look of panic on Torii's face, smiled, and said, "Just kidding. Have fun."

Torii's big moment ended a few minutes later when the next hitter grounded into a game-ending double play. Torii returned to the minor leagues a few days later, but the experience left a big impression on him. Just one day in the major leagues gave him a glimpse of what his future might hold if he continued to stay focused on his goal.

Now that he had a taste of the major leagues, nothing could stop him. For the next few years he bounced back and forth between the Twins and the minor leagues, playing better each time. Finally, in 2001 he became the Twins regular center fielder. He had a terrific season and earned a Gold Glove Award as the best center fielder in the American League.

Then, in 2002, Torii became a star. He started the season by getting hits in thirteen of his first fourteen games and was named American League Player of the Month for April. Keyed by Torii's play, the Twins looked as if they had a chance to win a division title.

Fans all over the league discovered how much they enjoyed watching Torii play, and the confident young man with the ready smile impressed everyone with his work habits and pleasant personality. In midsummer he became the first Twin elected to the starting lineup in the All-Star Game since Kirby Puckett in 1995.

Torii defeated such stars as Alex Rodriguez and Barry Bonds to win the Home Run Derby contest, but he saved his best for the game.

With two out in the bottom of the first, Barry Bonds of

the San Francisco Giants came to bat. He drove the ball deep to right center field.

Torii broke with the pitch, racing as far as he possibly could to his left. As he approached the nine-foot-high fence, he jumped.

Torii went up and just seemed to keep going, his head even with the top of the fence and his left arm and glove stretched high. He reached his arm up and back and over the fence.

At the very top of his leap, his glove wrapped around the ball. Then he landed on the ground, the ball in his glove. Bonds was out.

Torii ran back toward the infield, a big smile on his face, and exchanged a high five with right fielder Ichiro Suzuki. Barry Bonds couldn't believe Torii had caught the ball, and he stood between first and second base, incredulous.

With a big smile on his face, he waited, and as Torii ran past, Bonds embraced him and lifted him into the air, and both men smiled as the crowd stood and cheered.

Torii Hunter had done the impossible. Then again, he had been doing that his whole life.

Torii Hunter has gone on to have a terrific major-league career for the Twins and Los Angeles Angels of Anaheim, whom he joined as a free agent in 2008 after signing a five-year contract worth $90 million. Through the 2011 season he has earned nine Gold Glove Awards and made the All-Star team four times.

More important, however, is that Torii has been able to keep his commitment to his family and his community. As he promised himself, he has provided his father with help for his drug addiction, taken care of his wife and children, and bought his mother a new home. In 2000 he moved to Dallas, where he bought each of his three brothers a home on the same street so they can remain close and take care of one another. With his wife, Katrina, he started his own foundation, The Torii Hunter Project (www.toriihunterproj ect.com), a comprehensive, long-term effort to have an impact on youth in need in various parts of the United States, helping to build character and send kids to college. In 2007 he was awarded the Marvin Miller Man of the Year Award by the Baseball Players Association as the player in either league whose on-field performance and contributions to his community inspire others to higher levels of achievement.

He's come a long way from Pine Bluff.

SOURCES AND FURTHER READING

I create books from a variety of different research materials — books, magazine and newspaper articles, films and videos, and online sources.

If you would like to learn more about any of the ballplayers profiled in *From Hardships to Championships,* you may wish to start by asking your teacher or school or town librarian for help. They can probably show you how to find articles and online information. You might also want to check out the sources listed below. If your school or library doesn't have them, your local library might be able to borrow them from another library for you.

Happy reading and researching!

BABE RUTH

Christopher, Matt, and Glenn Stout. *Babe Ruth: Legends in Sports.* Boston: Little Brown, 2005.

Older readers might enjoy:

Creamer, Robert. *Babe Ruth: The Legend Comes to Life.* New York: Simon and Schuster, 1974.

Also see Babe's website, www.baberuth.com, and check

out the movies *The Babe Ruth Story* (1948), starring William Bendix, and *The Babe* (1992), starring John Goodman.

JIMMY PIERSALL

Piersall, Jim, and Al Hirshberg. *Fear Strikes Out: The Jimmy Piersall Story.* New York: Curtis Publishing, 1955.

Jimmy's biography does a wonderful job of describing his childhood and early baseball career. You might also want to find the movie version of the book, *Fear Strikes Out,* made in 1957 and starring Karl Malden and Anthony Perkins.

RON LeFLORE

LeFlore, Ron, with Jim Hawkins. *Breakout: From Prison to the Big Leagues.* New York: Harper and Row, 1978.

Ron's autobiography gives a detailed account of his upbringing, but due to some adult language and situations, is not appropriate for children under the age of fourteen. Published under the title *One in a Million: The Ron LeFlore Story,* a film of the same name starring LeVar Burton was made in 1978. You might catch it someday on television.

JOE TORRE

Torre, Joe, and Tom Verducci. *Chasing the Dream: My Life-long Journey to the World Series*. New York: Bantam Books, 1997.

———. *The Yankee Years*. New York: Doubleday, 2009.

Joe Torre's first autobiography goes into a great deal of detail about his early life, playing career, and first season as Yankee manager. *The Yankee Years* covers his entire career as manager of the Yankees. His website is www.joetorre .org.

TORII HUNTER

While there are several books for younger readers about Torii Hunter, they are out of date and do not go into much detail about his upbringing. You may want to look up current articles about Torii's career with the Los Angeles Angels of Anaheim, or look on YouTube to find some videos of some of Torii's fabulous plays. Also check out his website, www.toriihunterproject.org.

APPENDIX

BABE RUTH CAREER STATISTICS

FULL NAME: George Herman Ruth   DEATH: August 16, 1948

BORN: February 6, 1895

HEIGHT: 6'2"   WEIGHT: 215 lbs.

THROWS: Left   HITS: Left

PITCHING

YEAR	TEAM	ERA	W	L	G	IP	H	R	ER	BB	K
1914	BOSTON RED SOX	3.91	2	1	4	23.0	21	12	10	7	3
1915	BOSTON RED SOX	2.44	18	8	32	217.2	166	80	59	85	112
1916	BOSTON RED SOX	1.75	23	12	44	323.2	230	83	63	118	170
1917	BOSTON RED SOX	2.01	24	13	41	326.1	244	93	73	108	128
1918	BOSTON RED SOX	2.22	13	7	20	166.1	125	51	41	49	40
1919	BOSTON RED SOX	2.97	9	5	17	133.1	148	59	44	58	30
1920	NEW YORK YANKEES	4.50	1	0	1	4.0	3	4	2	2	0
1921	NEW YORK YANKEES	9.00	2	0	2	9.0	14	10	9	9	2

1930	New York Yankees	3.00	1	0	1	9.0	11	3	3	2	3
1933	New York Yankees	5.00	1	0	1	9.0	12	5	5	3	0
Totals:		2.28	94	46	163	1221.1	974	400	309	441	488

BATTING

YEAR	TEAM	AVG	G	AB	R	H	2B	3B	HR	RBI
1914	Boston Red Sox	.200	5	10	1	2	1	0	0	2
1915	Boston Red Sox	.315	42	92	16	29	10	1	4	21
1916	Boston Red Sox	.272	67	136	18	37	5	3	3	15
1917	Boston Red Sox	.325	52	123	14	40	6	3	2	12
1918	Boston Red Sox	.300	95	317	50	95	26	11	11	66
1919	Boston Red Sox	.322	130	432	103	139	34	12	29	114
1920	New York Yankees	.376	142	458	158	172	36	9	54	137
1921	New York Yankees	.378	152	540	177	204	44	16	59	171

Year	Team									
1922	New York Yankees	.315	110	406	94	128	24	8	35	99
1923	New York Yankees	.393	152	522	151	205	45	13	41	131
1924	New York Yankees	.378	153	529	143	200	39	7	46	121
1925	New York Yankees	.290	98	359	61	104	12	2	25	66
1926	New York Yankees	.372	152	495	139	184	30	5	47	146
1927	New York Yankees	.356	151	540	158	192	29	8	60	164
1928	New York Yankees	.323	154	536	163	173	29	8	54	142
1929	New York Yankees	.345	135	499	121	172	26	6	46	154
1930	New York Yankees	.359	145	518	150	186	28	9	49	153
1931	New York Yankees	.373	145	534	149	199	31	3	46	163
1932	New York Yankees	.341	133	457	120	156	13	5	41	137
1933	New York Yankees	.301	137	459	97	138	21	3	34	103

1934	New York Yankees	.288	125	365	78	105	17	4	22	84
1935	Boston Braves	.181	28	72	13	13	0	0	6	12
Totals:		.342	2503	8399	2174	2873	506	136	714	2213

JIMMY PIERSALL CAREER STATISTICS

FULL NAME: James Anthony Piersall

BORN: November 14, 1929

HEIGHT: 6'0"   WEIGHT: 170 lbs.

THROWS: Right   HITS: Right

BATTING

YEAR	TEAM	AVG	G	B	R	H	2B	3B	HR	RB
1950	BOSTON RED SOX	.286	6	7	4	2	0	0	0	0
1952	BOSTON RED SOX	.267	56	161	28	43	8	0	1	16
1953	BOSTON RED SOX	.272	151	585	76	159	21	9	3	52
1954	BOSTON RED SOX	.285	133	474	77	135	24	2	8	38
1955	BOSTON RED SOX	.283	149	515	68	146	25	5	13	62
1956	BOSTON RED SOX	.293	155	601	91	176	40	6	14	87
1957	BOSTON RED SOX	.261	151	609	103	159	27	5	19	63

1958	Boston Red Sox	.237	130	417	55	99	13	5	8	48
1959	Cleveland Indians	.246	100	317	42	78	13	2	4	30
1960	Cleveland Indians	.282	138	486	70	137	12	4	18	66
1961	Cleveland Indians	.322	121	484	81	156	26	7	6	40
1962	Washington Senators	.244	135	471	38	115	20	4	4	31
1963	Los Angeles Angels	.308	20	52	4	16	1	0	0	4
1963	Washington Senators	.245	29	94	9	23	1	0	1	5
1963	Los Angeles Angels	.194	40	124	13	24	4	1	1	10
1964	Los Angeles Angels	.314	87	255	28	80	11	0	2	13
1965	California Angels	.268	53	112	10	30	5	2	2	12
1966	California Angels	.211	75	123	14	26	5	0	0	14
1967	California Angels	.000	5	3	0	0	0	0	0	0
Totals:		**.272**	**1734**	**5890**	**811**	**1604**	**256**	**52**	**104**	**591**

RON LEFLORE CAREER STATISTICS

Full name: Ronald LeFlore

Born: June 16, 1948

Height: 6'0"   Weight: 200 lbs.

Throws: Right Hits: Right

BATTING

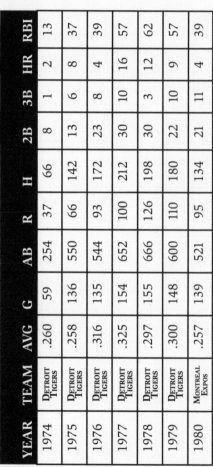

YEAR	TEAM	AVG	G	AB	R	H	2B	3B	HR	RBI
1974	Detroit Tigers	.260	59	254	37	66	8	1	2	13
1975	Detroit Tigers	.258	136	550	66	142	13	6	8	37
1976	Detroit Tigers	.316	135	544	93	172	23	8	4	39
1977	Detroit Tigers	.325	154	652	100	212	30	10	16	57
1978	Detroit Tigers	.297	155	666	126	198	30	3	12	62
1979	Detroit Tigers	.300	148	600	110	180	22	10	9	57
1980	Montreal Expos	.257	139	521	95	134	21	11	4	39

1981	Chicago White Sox	.246	82	337	46	83	10	4	0	24
1982	Chicago White Sox	.287	91	334	58	96	15	4	4	25
Totals:		**.288**	1099	4458	731	1283	172	57	59	353

JOE TORRE CAREER STATISTICS

FULL NAME: Joseph Paul Torre

BORN: July 18, 1940

HEIGHT: 6'2" WEIGHT: 212 lbs.

THROWS: Right   HITS: Right

BATTING

YEAR	TEAM	AVG	G	AB	R	H	2B	3B	HR	RBI
1960	MILWAUKEE BRAVES	.500	2	2	0	1	0	0	0	0
1961	MILWAUKEE BRAVES	.278	113	406	40	113	21	4	10	42
1962	MILWAUKEE BRAVES	.282	80	220	23	62	8	1	5	26
1963	MILWAUKEE BRAVES	.293	142	501	57	147	19	4	14	71
1964	MILWAUKEE BRAVES	.321	154	601	87	193	36	5	20	109
1965	MILWAUKEE BRAVES	.291	148	523	68	152	21	1	27	80
1966	ATLANTA BRAVES	.315	148	546	83	172	20	3	36	101

1967	Atlanta Braves	.277	135	477	67	132	18	1	20	68
1968	Atlanta Braves	.271	115	424	45	115	11	2	10	55
1969	St. Louis Cardinals	.289	159	602	72	174	29	6	18	101
1970	St. Louis Cardinals	.325	161	624	89	203	27	9	21	100
1971	St. Louis Cardinals	.363	161	634	97	230	34	8	24	137
1972	St. Louis Cardinals	.289	149	544	71	157	26	6	11	81
1973	St. Louis Cardinals	.287	141	519	67	149	17	2	13	69
1974	St. Louis Cardinals	.282	147	529	59	149	28	1	11	70
1975	New York Mets	.247	114	361	33	89	16	3	6	35
1976	New York Mets	.306	114	310	36	95	10	3	5	31
1977	New York Mets	.176	26	51	2	9	3	0	1	9
Totals:		.297	2209	7874	996	2342	344	59	252	1185

MANAGER

Year	Team	W		%	FINISH	
1977	New York Mets	49	68	.419	6	
1978	New York Mets	66	96	.407	6	
1979	New York Mets	63	99	.389	6	
1980	New York Mets	67	95	.414	5	
1981	New York Mets	17	34	.333	5	
1981	New York Mets	24	28	.462	4	
1982	Atlanta Braves	89	73	.549	1	
1983	Atlanta Braves	88	74	.543	2	
1984	Atlanta Braves	80	82	.494	3	
1990	St. Louis Cardinals	24	34	.414	6	
1991	St. Louis Cardinals	84	78	.519	2	

Year	Team	W	L	Pct	Rank	
1992	St. Louis Cardinals	83	79	.512	3	
1993	St. Louis Cardinals	87	75	.537	3	
1994	St. Louis Cardinals	53	61	.465	3	
1995	St. Louis Cardinals	20	27	.426	4	
1996	New York Yankees	92	70	.568	1	World Series Champs
1997	New York Yankees	96	66	.593	2	
1998	New York Yankees	114	48	.704	1	World Series Champs
1999	New York Yankees	98	64	.605	1	World Series Champs
2000	New York Yankees	87	74	.540	1	World Series Champs
2001	New York Yankees	95	65	.594	1	AL Pennant
2002	New York Yankees	103	58	.640	1	
2003	New York Yankees	101	61	.623	1	AL Pennant
2004	New York Yankees	101	61	.623	1	

2005	New York Yankees		95	67	.586	1
2006	New York Yankees		97	65	.599	1
2007	New York Yankees		94	68	.580	2
2008	Los Angeles Dodgers		84	78	.519	1
2009	Los Angeles Dodgers		95	67	.586	1
2010	Los Angeles Dodgers	NL	80	82	.494	4

Total 2,326 1997 .538

TORII HUNTER CAREER STATISTICS

FULL NAME: Torii Kedar Hunter

BORN: July 18, 1975

HEIGHT: 6'2" WEIGHT: 225 lbs.

THROWS: Right HITS: Right

BATTING

YEAR	TEAM	AVG	G	AB	R	H	2B	3B	HR	RBI
1997	MINNESOTA TWINS	.000	1	0	0	0	0	0	0	0
1998	MINNESOTA TWINS	.235	6	17	0	4	1	0	0	2
1999	MINNESOTA TWINS	.255	135	384	52	98	17	2	9	35
2000	MINNESOTA TWINS	.280	99	336	44	94	14	7	5	44
2001	MINNESOTA TWINS	.261	148	564	82	147	32	5	27	92
2002	MINNESOTA TWINS	.289	148	561	89	162	37	4	29	94
2003	MINNESOTA TWINS	.250	154	581	83	145	31	4	26	102

2004	Minnesota Twins	.271	138	520	79	141	37	0	23	81
2005	Minnesota Twins	.269	98	372	63	100	24	1	14	56
2006	Minnesota Twins	.278	147	557	86	155	21	2	31	98
2007	Minnesota Twins	.287	160	600	94	172	45	1	28	107
2008	Los Angeles Angels	.278	146	551	85	153	37	2	21	78
2009	Los Angeles Angels	.299	119	451	74	135	26	1	22	90
2010	Los Angeles Angels	.281	152	573	76	161	36	0	23	90
2011	Los Angeles Angels	.262	156	580	80	152	24	2	23	82
Totals:		.274	1807	6647	987	1819	382	31	281	1051

PLAYING FOR THE LOVE OF THE GAME!

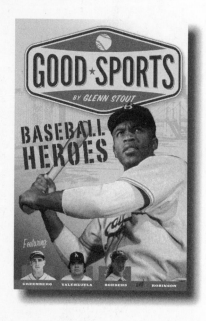

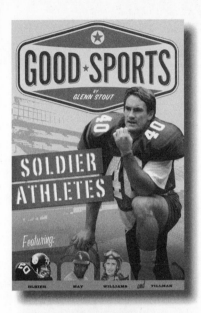

FACT OR FICTION? READ THESE AWESOME NOVELS ABOUT SPORTS AND ATHLETES.

PEAK

The emotional, tension-filled story of a fourteen-year-old boy's attempt to be the youngest person to reach the top of Mount Everest.

TANGERINE

In Tangerine County, Florida, weird is normal. Lightning strikes at the same time every day, a sinkhole swallows a local school, and Paul the geek finds himself adopted into the toughest group around: the middle school soccer team.

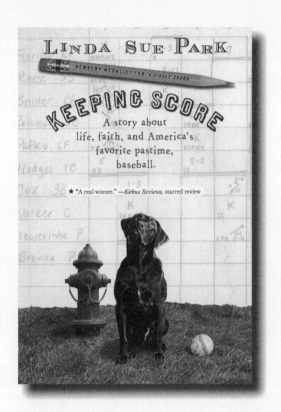

KEEPING SCORE

Nine-year-old Maggie learns a lot about baseball and life in this historical novel set during the Korean War and the Dodgers' 1951 season.

FIND MORE FUN AND FUNNY BIOGRAPHIES IN THE LIVES OF . . . SERIES.

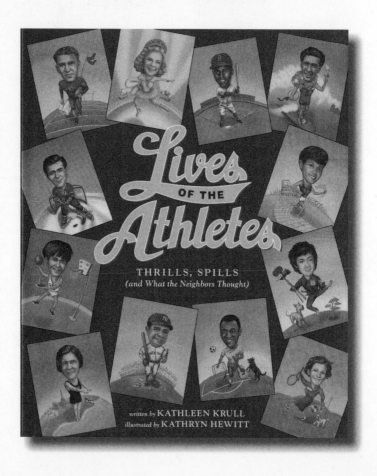

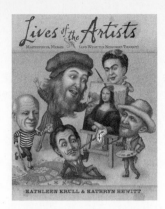

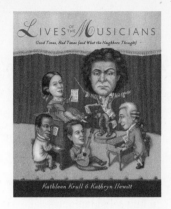

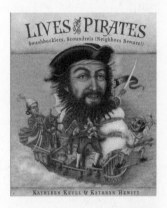

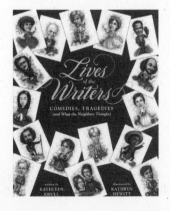

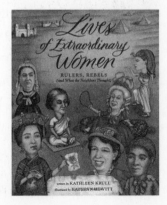

ABOUT THE AUTHOR

When Glenn Stout was growing up outside a small town in central Ohio, he never dreamed that he would become a writer. Then reading changed his life. As a kid, Glenn played baseball, basketball, and football, but baseball was always his favorite sport. Glenn studied poetry and creative writing in college and has had many different jobs, including selling minor-league baseball tickets, cleaning offices, grading papers for a college, and painting houses. He also worked as a construction worker and a librarian. Glenn started writing professionally while he was working at the Boston Public Library and has been a full-time writer since 1993. Under the auspices of Matt Christopher, Glenn wrote forty titles in the Matt Christopher sports biography series, and every year he edits *The Best American Sports Writing* collection. Some of Glenn's other books include *Fenway 1912, Red Sox Century, Yankees Century, Nine Months at Ground Zero,* and *Young Woman and the Sea: How Trudy Ederle Conquered the English Channel and Inspired the World*. He has written or edited more than eighty books, and also works as a consultant and editor, giving advice to other writers.

Glenn is a citizen of both the United States and Canada and lives on Lake Champlain in Vermont with his wife, daughter, two cats, two dogs, and a rabbit. He writes in a messy office in his basement, and when he isn't working, he likes to ski, skate, hike in the woods, kayak on the lake, take photographs, and read.